THE POSTAGE STAMPS
OF GREAT BRITAIN

PART TWO: REVISED EDITION

THE POSTAGE STAMPS
OF GREAT BRITAIN

PART TWO: REVISED EDITION

The Perforated Line-Engraved Issues

Edited by
W. R. D. WIGGINS

with additions by
C. GARDINER-HILL
and numerous new illustrations by
G. V. ELTRINGHAM

THE ROYAL PHILATELIC SOCIETY LONDON
41 Devonshire Place London W1
1962

© *The Royal Philatelic Society London*

Printed at the University Press Glasgow
by Robert MacLehose and Company Limited

First Edition 1937
Second Edition 1962

Preface

THE preparation of the second edition of Great Britain Part II, based on the late J. B. Seymour's classic work, has involved over ten years of research and the Society is indebted to those who have given so much of their time to this important task.

It will be remembered that as soon as the second edition of Part I, completed by Seymour shortly before his death, was published in 1950 an Editorial Committee was formed to work on Part II. It was decided to confine this Volume to the Perforated Line-Engraved issues, seeing that Seymour had closed the second edition of Part I with the last of the Imperforates; the second half of the first edition of Part II, dealing with the Embossed and Surface-printed issues of Queen Victoria, was combined with the Edward VII issues to make a new Part III. This was published in 1954, and Part IV, dealing with the issues of George V, followed in 1957.

The Publications Committee would like to take this opportunity, on behalf of the Society, of thanking Mr F. C. Holland, Dr H. W. Eddison, Dr W. R. D. Wiggins and Dr C. Gardiner-Hill for the interest and advice they gave as members of the Editorial Committee which originally planned this second edition of Part II. Dr Gardiner-Hill has brought up to date as far as practicable the first two chapters dealing with the Archer perforations and the Die I perforated, and Dr Wiggins has completely revised and rewritten the chapters dealing with the One Penny Die II perforated. In both these sections much of Seymour has survived as he wrote it, and all his work on the constant varieties and re-entries, with his drawings, has been incorporated in the new lists.

The placing of the illustrations immediately above the descriptions in these new lists will no doubt be a welcome feature, and in this connection the Publications Committee would like to thank Mr Eltringham for his devoted work in providing over eight hundred new drawings to illustrate the more important re-entries and constant varieties which now appear in the lists. Their thanks are also due to Mr Robson Lowe, who has co-operated with Dr Gardiner-Hill in bringing the first two chapters up to date in addition to contributing much original work. He has also provided a number of the blocks, including the illustrations of the combs used by Archer.

5

The Publications Committee would also call attention to the great trouble taken by Dr Wiggins and Mr Lowe in obtaining for reproduction photographs of top right-hand corner stamps (AL or AX) to illustrate the various types dealt with in the book. They will be found on *Plates 5, 8* and *9*. The comparative illustrations of Dies I and II on *Plate 6* and *Plate 7* have been reproduced from Wright and Creeke. The material for *Plates 1, 2, 3, 4, 10* and *11* has been provided by Mr Lowe.

The chapters on the Perforated Twopence and the Plate Numbers have been left more or less as Seymour wrote them. The publication after Seymour's death of the late Dr Osborne's work on the Twopence has established him as the recognised authority on those sections, and the Plate Numbers can safely be left to speak for themselves.

October, 1962

JOHN EASTON
ARNOLD M. STRANGE
Publications Committee

Contents

Illustrations

8

Chapter One

Early Roulettes and Perforations

PRIVATE AND UNOFFICIAL SEPARATIONS

Stamps privately rouletted by hand are known from 1841, this apparently having been done for convenience with a small steel spur-wheel. Genuine examples of these are not common but they can only be regarded as curiosities and they should not be confused with the unused stamps rouletted by Archer. Covers have been found in original archives bearing stamps with crude pin perforations. A cutting machine which severed sheets into vertical strips was in private use in Southampton in 1847; the result may only be identified when the stamp is so mis-shapen that it is a rhomboid and not an oblong. A Mr Bemrose of Derby invented a rouletting machine and sent samples of his work on plain paper to Rowland Hill.

An unused block from Plate 10 of the One Penny red-brown, perforated 11–12 by the trial machine used by Perkins Bacon for Antigua, Bahamas, Barbados, etc., about 1861–62, is known; there is a block with the same perforation used at Hereford in the Royal Collection.

Presumably these perforations were unofficial and it is not known when they were made. There was a considerable number of sheets from Plate 10 unissued, both with and without gum.

ARCHER ROULETTES

A scheme for the perforation of stamps to facilitate their separation was first brought to the notice of the postal authorities by an enterprising business man, Henry Archer. He pointed out that having to separate the 'postage labels' by cutting or tearing, gave trouble, and caused great loss of time to users having an extensive correspondence, and also to postal employees. He invented his first perforating machine in 1847, which was actually a rouletting machine.

Archer claimed that his plan would greatly convenience the public, and on the 1st October, 1847, it was submitted to the Postmaster-General, who referred it to the post office technical department in order to ascertain the efficacy of the machine. The report being favourable, it was forwarded to the Commissioners of Stamps and Taxes with a recommendation to adopt the system if they considered it advisable. Ormond Hill was consulted, and after making enquiries he gave his opinion that,

9

on public grounds, it was desirable to adopt the plan, and consequently Archer was asked to have two more perforating machines made. At his own expense Archer made arrangements with a mechanical engineer named Addenbrooke to construct them.

The first machine punctured the paper with lines of short cuts made by two rollers in succession. One carried thirteen small spur wheels, the width of a stamp apart, to puncture the vertical columns, and the other with wheels the length of a stamp apart for the horizontal rows. The trial was a failure, as it was found that the spurs so wore the table on which the sheets were laid that the process was too costly and uncertain. The attempt at perforation by rollers was therefore abandoned.

The second machine, consisting of lancet-shaped blades, working on the fly-press principle and piercing the paper with a series of cuts, was abandoned for the same reason. This method is known as rouletting, and Archer's roulette gauged about 11½.

The trials were made on plain paper, and were not carried out under Government supervision. The few sheets of stamps known to have been experimented on were probably bought by Archer, and were not put into circulation. Known unused examples are from Plates 70 and 71, and are extremely scarce.

ARCHER'S PERFORATION 16

Archer continued his experiments, and devised a machine to perforate the sheets with small holes between the stamps. Instead of two single machines, a double punching machine was constructed to perforate two series of sheets placed side by side, and ten sheets could be perforated at one time.

The perforating comb consisted of a long horizontal row of steel pins with 26 short vertical lines of pins, equally spaced, making an allowance for the margins of the sheets which lay side by side. The pins descended into corresponding holes in a metal plate, and the comb, in one operation, perforated the top and sides of one row of stamps. The sheets were then mechanically moved forward the distance between the rows, and a second operation perforated the bottom line and the sides of the next row. This was repeated until the whole sheet was completed. There were sixteen pins to each 2 cm.

The first trials of this third machine, which underwent many alterations, were made at Perkins, Bacon & Petch's works in December, 1848, but they failed through the matrices clogging by reason of the dampness of the gum, and also through the irregular alignment of the stamps. Archer was dissatisfied with the treatment of the machine by Perkins, Bacon & Petch, although J. B. Bacon stated that every facility had been given for a fair trial, and eventually he ceased to communicate with them. Ormond Hill consulted De La Rue, who expressed the opinion that the machine would not have clogged if the gum had been perfectly dry. Eventually Archer removed the machine from the printers to make some alterations suggested by Hill and De La Rue and have it put in order.

After the machine had been improved by adjusting mechanism which enabled the movements to be regulated to the slightly different sizes of the sheets, caused by unequal contraction from damping, it was transferred to Somerset House on January 9th, 1850, and following an extended series of trials was approved by the Commissioners of Inland Revenue in August 1850.

In their report, dated May 21st, 1852, the Select Committee appointed by the Government was unanimously of the opinion that the perforating of postage stamps would be of great advantage to the public, and that Archer's machine should be purchased. A very inadequate sum was offered him, which he indignantly refused, and in June 1853 he received £4000 for all his rights. All the experiments with the third machine were carried out under Government supervision by Perkins, Bacon & Petch, and afterwards at Somerset House. Archer's experiments terminated at the end of 1850. Some 5000 trial sheets were made, most of which, owing to imperfections, were destroyed. As Alphabet II was only introduced in March 1852 the trial sheets obviously had the small check letters of Alphabet I.

Due chiefly to the researches of Dr C. Gardiner-Hill and Mr Robson Lowe a lot of information is now available in regard to the Archer Perforated 16 Die I. In all 137 dated covers and 1345 single stamps have been examined, representing a large proportion of those still in existence, and large pieces of Plates 96 and 98 have led to the identification of four combs. The fact that these four combs measure 23 mm vertically, whereas the normal 1854 comb measures 23½ mm, is a certain identification, and replaces the old custom of assuming that all Alphabet I perforated 16 were perforated on Archer machines, and even by Henry Archer himself.

It is also now possible to allocate these stamps to their correct plates. Sheets from Plates 92 to 101 were given to Archer to demonstrate his invention, and it can only be assumed that all experimental printings either by himself or Somerset House were carried out with sheets from these plates as, with only a few exceptions, all stamps can be identified as belonging to this group. There are in existence an unused block from Plate 71, pairs from Plates 8 and 105, and singles from Plates 79, 90 and 91, and there is no reason to believe that the perforations are faked. Unfortunately these few stamps cannot be dated as they are not on covers.

The perforated stamps from the main group, Plates 92–101, with the exception of two covers posted in London in August, are first found in the last three months of 1850. The majority of these were posted in the West Country. They are also found in the first six months of 1851 when many of them still come from the West Country, but postings in London are much more numerous. They are not found in 1852 but they appear again in the last six months of 1853, when more are posted in London than elsewhere. They are also found in the first six months of 1854 when the majority were posted in London in February, March and April.

The 1853–54 examples are almost certainly remainders from the stock perforated by Archer in 1850.

There is an interesting retouch on TG of Plate 94, in the right hand corner, N.W. of the G square, which became progressively visible as the plate showed signs of wear; it does not appear on the Imprimatur. As this plate was used by Archer for his experiments it is possible that copies will be found perforated 16. It was discovered by Mr Hans Pinkus.*

Plate 95 was finished on June 21st, 1849, but was defective and was not submitted for approval. On January 3rd, 1850, Perkins Bacon altered Plate 100 to Plate 95 'in place of Plate 95 which was spoiled', and this was approved on January 7th.† A new Plate 100 was finished on February 14th. There is no evidence to connect the first Plate 95 with the plate about which Archer complained so bitterly in his memorial of May 1850 as being the wrong size.

As the following tables with the quantities of stamps identified from each plate show, all the plates handed over to Archer were used during the four years.

1850

94–1; 97–3; 98–3; 99–7; 100–8; 101–1

1851

92–2; 93–1; 94–2; 95–1; 96–7; 97–2; 98–3; 100–5; 101–3

1853

92–2; 93–7; 94–5; 96–1; 97–4; 98–6; 99–3; 100–1; 101–1

1854

93–9; 94–7; 95–3; 96–3; 97–7; 98–5; 99–3; 100–16; 101–5

UNDATED

92–11; 93–91; 94–84; 95–29; 96–239; 97–123; 98–338; 99–89; 100–209; 101–42

---

* Great Britain Philatelist, Vol 1, No 2, p. 26.
† The Line Engraved Postage Stamps of Great Britain, by Sir E. D. Bacon, Vol. II. p. 274.

There is in the Royal Collection a sheet of paper perforated by Archer's third machine which shows all perforations in perfect alignment; this is referred to below as Comb C. But as there are blocks in existence showing variations in the perforation it is certain that other combs were used.

Plate 98 has been identified with three different combs:

Comb A. The bottom two holes between the vertical B and C rows are joined together. There is also a pin out of alignment at the bottom of the vertical D row. Although known as the 'bent pin' this is a misnomer; the hole is clear cut, whereas there would have been no hole if the pin had been bent. The holes are out of alignment, especially vertically. Comb A is illustrated on *Plate 2.*

Comb B. The 'bent pin' variety is present, but there is no fusion of the bottom two holes, and the holes are out of alignment. The cover partly illustrated on *Plate 2* was posted in 1854.

The horizontal line of holes in this comb does not coincide with the vertical line, as the following diagram shows:

Combs A, C and D   Comb B

Comb C. No evidence of either variety. The alignment is perfect.

The second experiment (or possibly the so-called Napier trial made in 1853) is believed to be Comb B, and the third experiment Comb A. If this is correct, then Comb C may be a second trial on the Napier machine.

Comb D. Plate 96 has been identified showing that a fourth comb (D) was used. In this the alignment is perfect, but the holes are larger and mint blocks tend to sever.

In Comb D, illustrated on *Plate 3*, there is a wavy appearance between the vertical J, K and L rows. Generally, the vertical perforation (i.e. the teeth of the comb) was too long and caused a bad corner at the junction of the stamps. This is quite distinct on the stamps JG, JH, JK, KI and KL in the illustration.

It is possible that Archer's first experiment in perforating was made with this machine.

The irregularities which appear on these combs are also found on stamps with Alphabet II. The vertical measurement also establishes the fact that the Archer comb was used to perforate the Twopence Blue Plate 4 cancelled with the Somerset House Inspector's mark.

Among the 1,500 used and 340 unused stamps with Alphabet I corner letters perforated 16 examined by Dr Gardiner-Hill and Mr Lowe it was noted that none showed any portion of the sheet margins. It is not known whether Archer's combs showed the extension of one horizontal perforation hole in the left and right sheet margins, but all those stamps perforated on the Napier machines show this feature.

Many stamps with trial perforations are of poor colour; a dull, flat shade of brown. These may have been sheets rejected for normal issue owing to their colour.

Stamps with Archer's perforation also exist with inverted watermarks, and the McGowan collection contained one example used in the Crimea in 1854.

NAPIER PERFORATING MACHINES

The Government acquired Archer's patents in June 1853, and steps were immediately taken to provide suitable machines. These were constructed by David Napier & Sons, and some months later were installed at Somerset House. Trial perforations from these machines are known.

Perforation 16

Stamps with corner letters from Alphabet I, which were obsolete by this time, have been described on pages 11 to 13. Those stamps with Alphabet II can only be distinguished from the normal issue by the date, which must precede 28th January, 1854, when the officially perforated stamps were brought into use. Such covers are extremely rare. Those stamps that have been plated are from one or other of the plates which are known officially perforated. It is possible that all perforated stamps from plates 160 and 161 are trials (see page 27).

Stamps with corner letters from Alphabet II cancelled with the Birmingham duplex date-stamp in January 1851 are errors of date for 1855 or more, probably 1856. The stamps are usually from Reserve Plate 2.

Perforation 14

Stamps with corner letters from Alphabet I are known from Plates 74 and 113, the former in the poor colour usually associated with the Archer trials, the latter on thick ungummed paper. These are probably from waste sheets used at the end of 1854 at Somerset House for trials on the Napier machines with the comb with the perforation gauge 14. Marginal pieces show an extension of the horizontal perforation by one hole in the side margins. It is probable that trials were made with this comb on stamps with corner letters from Alphabet II. If these are to be identified with certainty they must be on covers dated before 1st January, 1855. It is possible that all stamps from Plates 192 and 193 with this perforation are trials (see the Table of Rarity on page 27).

THE TREASURY ROULETTE

Among the trial roulettes there is included a variety in which the stamps were partly divided by an instrument which made continuous serpentine cuts. These instruments are said to have been used at the Treasury when Mr Gladstone was Chancellor of the Exchequer, and are popularly known as the Gladstone, or Treasury, roulette. (See *Plate 1*.)

It appears that more than one instrument was in use as 'wave-lengths' of different sizes are to be found. In some examples the severing lines are continuous but in the majority the centres of the 'crests' or 'hollows' show tiny uncut portions which had to be severed in order to separate the stamps.

The roulette does not always appear on all four sides of the stamp and it would appear that the rouletting instrument was only applied to large blocks, possibly quarter sheets of five horizontal rows, as usually the horizontal E, J and O rows are imperforate at the foot and the horizontal F, K and P rows are imperforate at the top.

Sir E. D. Bacon mentions a vertical pair, and a strip of four of the One Penny VR official stamps rouletted by this method, which are in the Royal collection, and these examples have been obliterated with an official trial cancellation, which was undoubtedly applied at the Treasury. Stamps with this roulette are not usually found unused although one copy is said to exist, and most of the known examples have the London District obliteration.

Covers or pieces with unsevered pairs exist. Dated copies range from December 17th, 1852, to May 1854. The used examples are only known on the One Penny with Alphabet II, which was then in use.

Chapter Two

Third Issue of One Penny Perforated

OFFICIAL PERFORATIONS

The issue of officially perforated stamps began with the One Penny on the 28th and with the Twopence on the 31st January, 1854.

The Napier machines were constructed with combs only one sheet wide, and usually five sheets were perforated together. They were at first worked by hand, and later by steam. The guide marks on the upper and lower margins enabled the sheets to be centred on the machine, and normally they were fed in with the A horizontal row uppermost, which gave a vertically perforated margin at the bottom. The position, however, was frequently reversed.

The combs consisted of a plate set with projecting steel pins with flat ends, which fitted into a bed with sharp-edged holes to correspond. They were interchangeable so could be replaced when repairs were necessary.

At first, the gauge measured 16 pins to 2 cm, but as this made the sheets too delicate to handle without breaking, towards the end of 1854 the number of pins was reduced to 14, and from the beginning of 1855 the sheets were perforated for some time 16 and 14 concurrently. Afterwards only the 14 gauge was used, except that at the end of 1857 a small number of sheets of the One Penny and Twopence were perforated 16.

In spite of complaints the alignment of the plate impressions was always faulty and the irregular stretching of the paper, caused by the necessary damping of the sheets, could not be controlled. Consequently when the comb was adjusted to the first line of stamps the successive columns gradually got out of place, and towards the last rows stamps were cut into on one side. An improvement to make the comb adjustable did not entirely overcome the difficulty. The proportion of 'off centre' stamps of the 1854–55 period is very great.

BROKEN PIN VARIETIES

Perforation varieties caused by broken pins are not unusual in the single copy but it is now possible to follow the development through the plates. The comb of the perforating machine perforated one horizontal row on the sheet at a time. A missing pin left a small portion of paper between the stamps imperforate so that a jagged tear resulted, damaging at least one of the stamps when two were separated.

A missing pin in the horizontal perforation results in the same variety occurring at the top and bottom of the same stamp and is repeated in

16

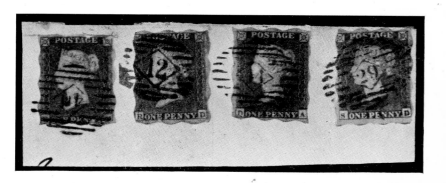

TREASURY ROULETTES

[*Plate 1*]

SHORT STAMPS

One pin   Normal   Two Pins

ARCHER COMB A: PLATE 98

Note joined perforation holes between vertical B and C rows and bent hole between
D and E rows

ARCHER COMB B: PLATE 98

Note bent hole between BD and BE

[Plate 2]

ARCHER COMB D: PLATE 96

With large holes

ARCHER COMB D: PLATE 96

Note larger holes: also the wavy appearance of the vertical perforations between the J, K and L rows

[*Plate 3*]

Variety 1   Variety 2

Variety 3   Variety 4

Variety 5

BROKEN PINS

[Plate 4]

the same vertical row throughout the sheet. In the vertical perforation it is repeated in every stamp in the same vertical row throughout.

When the issue of perforated One Penny stamps began on 28th January, 1854, the plates in use were 155, 157 and 160 to 177. The earliest plate on which a broken pin has been noted is 155. Plates 155, 160, 161, 162, 164, 165, 167, 168, 169, 170, 171, 172, 174, 175, 180, 181 and 183 had been defaced in August 1854. The first variety has been noted on Plates 155 to 180 and the first state of the second variety on Plates 162 to 179. This suggests that these breaks occurred in the middle of 1854.

As more than one comb was in use at a time, the broken pin varieties do not show on each sheet and the number of perforation varieties is not the same proportionally as the number of stamps examined. See *Plate 4*.

The first variety. This is the missing 14th perforation from the top of the stamps between the vertical A and B rows. It has been noted on Plates 155, 162, 166, 167, 169, 174, 175, 176, 177, 178 and 180. An analysis suggests that Plate 162 is the most common; Plates 174, 175, and 177 are about six times rarer than Plate 162; and the rest about three times rarer.

The second variety. This shows various pins missing on the marginal side of the vertical L row. There are six states (the perforation holes are counted from the top of each stamp).

State 1: 16th and 18th pins missing; noted on Plates 155, 171.

State 2: 15th, 16th, and 18th pins missing; noted on Plates 162, 166, 169, 177, 178, 179.

State 3: 10th, 14th, 15th and 18th pins missing ; noted on Plates 164, 169, 171, 173, 175, 177, 178, 179.

State 4: 10th, 14th, 15th, 16th and 18th pins missing; noted on Plate 155.

State 5: 5th, 10th, 14th to 18th pins missing; noted on Plates 169, 174.

State 6: 5th, 8th, 10th, 14th to 18th pins missing; noted on Plates 162, 169, 175, 183.

The third variety. This occurs in two states in the vertical A row:

State 1: 5th horizontal pin from the left missing; noted on Plate 197.

State 2: An additional pin missing on the left, the second vertical; noted on Plates 191, 193 and 197.

The first state is much rarer than the second.

The fourth variety. This occurs in two states on the vertical L row:

State 1: 5th horizontal pin from the left missing; noted on Plate R4.

State 2: Both 5th and 6th horizontal pins missing; noted on Plates 196, 200, 202, 204, R1, R3, R4, R5 and R6.

The fifth variety. This is rare; it is found in the vertical A row. It has been noted on Plates 193 to 198, 200, 201, 202, R1 to R6, and covers

B

are dated January and February 1855. Twelve perforations are missing; the size of the remaining holes varies from the normal to the largest (see *Plate 4*) but sometimes the punctures are blind. Usually the sheet margin has been removed by cutting.

These varieties may be found on the opposite side of the sheet when the sheet was fed into the perforating machine inverted (T row first). Numerically the inverted variety is twenty times rarer than the normal.

SHORT STAMPS

Stamps which are shorter than normal are commonly found from the horizontal A row and more rarely from the T row. Perforation 16 normally provides 19 pins on the vertical side but approximately 27·5% of stamps lettered A in the lower left corner have only 18 or more rarely 17 perforations. See *Plate 2*.

The imperforate sheet was fed into the perforating machine and the first row perforated on three sides. If the horizontal perforation touched the design of the stamp then the second row was adjusted by one or two holes which made the top row in the sheet short.

If the sheet of stamps was fed into the perforating machine inverted, the T row would be short. Such varieties will be found in 5% of stamps lettered T in the lower left corner.

Short stamps will be found in nearly the same proportion when first perforated 14 and have been noted among all stamps perforated at Somerset House on this machine up to 1878.

Watermark Small Crown: Die I: Alphabet II

The stamps of this issue appeared in many shades of warm red-brown to brick-red, and yellowish-brown to orange-brown. An uncommon colour is plum, which, however, is accentuated by the deep blueing of the paper. A rare shade of Die I is a rich lake-red, usually only associated with the large crown watermark, Die II. There are few variations of shades in the prevailing red-brown of Die II, which sometimes shows a tendency towards an orange-brown.

At this period the gum was improved by the introduction of gelatine.

PLATES 155 to 157, 160 to 204, R1 to R6

The first officially perforated sheets were from Plates 155, 157 and 160 onwards with Alphabet II. The intervening Plates 156, 158 and 159 had been defaced in August 1853, and the stock of stamps from these was probably exhausted before the Napier machines were used.

When perforation was introduced there was a stock of sheets at Somerset House from about twenty plates many of which were then at press, and consequently stamps from these plates, which had been issued imperforate, are also known perforated. The identification of examples of both states is possible. Identified examples of the earlier of these plates are usually imperforate, and perforated examples from some of them are rare. Re-entries and other plate varieties are very scarce.

RE-ENTRIES and CONSTANT VARIETIES

The following list contains all the re-entries and constant varieties described by the late J. B. Seymour in the first edition of this book; it also includes his thirty-six illustrations. Of these Seymour suggested identifications for four.

Subsequent research by Dr Gardiner-Hill and Mr C. W. Meredith has led to the identification of all but four: two illustrated re-entries and two varieties not illustrated (LL and TB). Dr Gardiner-Hill has in addition identified twenty-five new re-entries. These are included in the list, together with some of the many varieties he has plated.

The list also includes, and illustrates, the diadem flaw in DC of Plate 166, pointed out by Dr Gardiner-Hill, and the diadem flaw on Plate 196, affecting KB, LB and MB, discovered by Mr Lowe.

PLATE 155

AB Check letters faint; spot in margin under Y of PENNY (may also be found imperforate)

AG Re-entry in the upper squares, value, and G square

BB First state: re-entry in both the upper and first B squares (may also be found imperforate)

BB Second state: check letters faint; marks of re-entry in the squares, POSTAGE, and value (may also be found imperforate)

BD Slight re-entry in the upper corners and POSTAGE

HA Slight re-entry in POSTAGE and value; A open

RJ Re-entry in the N.E. square: vertical line near the frame line in the R square; horizontal line above J

Note: See p. 26 for a note on the general repairs of this plate

PLATE 157

AA   Re-entry in the upper squares and under NN of PENNY (may also be found imperforate)

BA   Re-entry in the upper squares (may also be found imperforate)

MJ   Re-entry N.E. square and top line

SJ   Re-entry POSTAGE, N.W. square and above

PLATE 158

RD   A well-registered double impression in the upper squares and POSTAGE

PLATE 160

AA   Slight re-entry in the upper squares, POSTAGE and value, from a third plate

PLATE 162

KJ   Lines below and to right of J square

NA   Horizontal line below the A square

OK   Horizontal line just above O square on margin

RK   Diagonal mark through the frame line in the K square

PLATE 163

TA   Re-entry in the N.E. corner; blob below A square

PLATE 164

ME   Horizontal line under M square (See Plate 175)

PLATE 165

MI   Horizontal line under M square

PLATE 166

DC   Long flaw coinciding with lower edge of diadem (see p. 19)

PLATE 167

HF   Marks in A of POSTAGE and below

MF   Horizontal line under M square

NA   Horizontal line below A square

SH   Clear re-entry in the upper squares, POSTAGE, and value (may also be found imperforate)

PLATE 168

ME Horizontal line under M square

PLATE 169

JJ Horizontal line below first J square

ME Horizontal line below M square

PLATE 171

FD Two marks on chin

MK Vertical mark in M square and horizontal line beneath

TI Clear double impression of the value, and in I square (may be Plate 170, which has been reported in two states)

PLATE 173

PH Horizontal line under P square

PLATE 174

DA Re-entry in POSTAGE, upper squares and above

HA First state: re-entry in the N.W. square; horizontal line close to top of frame-line

HA Second state: slight re-entry in POSTAGE and value

LF Slight re-entry in the N.E. square, and POSTAGE

QH Mark in and above N.W. square

PLATE 175

LE Diagonal line below Y of PENNY

MA Horizontal stroke under the corner of the M square; other stamps from the M row often show a similar mark; the length of the stroke varies

PLATE 177

KK Several dots below PENNY

ML Line through P of POSTAGE

PLATE 178

FH Diagonal mark in H square

PLATE 179

SD Mark in E of POSTAGE

Note: The Q of this plate has a long tail

PLATE 181

SH Two blurred marks to left of S square

PLATE 183

MI Horizontal line under M square

PLATE 184

AH Diagonal scratch extending from lower margin into O of ONE

PF Re-entry POSTAGE and upper squares

SL Blob below left corner of s square

PLATE 185

SE Re-entry upper squares

Note: See p. 26 for note on framed stamps from this plate

PLATE 186

MH Horizontal line under M square

PI Re-entry in value and both letter squares

QB Slight re-entry in the value and lower margin

RB Re-entry upper squares

PLATE 187

CJ Re-entry in upper squares: top side lines of squares weak; POSTAGE thin

FL Marked re-entry upper squares and POSTAGE; top lines of upper squares faint.

MI Horizontal line under M square

PLATE 188

BI Re-entry in both the upper and B squares, POSTAGE and value

JF Re-entry in upper squares, E of POSTAGE and J square; bottom line of J square missing

MG Horizontal line under M square

PLATE 189

BA Remarkable re-entry of the whole value extending down to the upper tablet of CA; off-centred examples of BA or CA are necessary to show it

CA See BA

IL Re-entry in upper squares

RA Slight double impression in the value, and below; E and PE of ONE PENNY run into the margin

PLATE 190

KA Re-entry POSTAGE and value

PLATE 191

RK Vertical stroke to left of K

SG Re-entry POSTAGE and upper squares

PLATE 192

AI   Re-entry in the upper squares, POSTAGE, and value

HL   Top serif of L double

PLATE 193

HB   Re-entry in POSTAGE

EG   E double

EL   Two marks in L square to left of L

TH   T double

PLATE 194

LG   Slight re-entry in the upper squares

MG   Horizontal line under M square

MI   M double

PA   Re-entry POSTAGE and value

PLATE 195

CK   Blob of colour on left margin opposite neck

KL   Horizontal mark below L square

LC   Two dots in L square to right of L

LJ   Blob on left margin opposite nose

MJ   Horizontal line under M square

NL   Strong re-entry in the upper squares; traces of double impressions in POSTAGE and value

PLATE 196

KB   Plate flaw on diadem (see p. 19)

LB   See KB

MB   See KB

MK   Diagonal line below M square

NK   Diagonal line touching N.W. square

QF   Numerous marks in both letter squares; top serif of F faint

RF   Re-entry POSTAGE and upper squares

PLATE 197

DC   Blob above N.W. square

EK   Thin horizontal line in E square

FA   Mark on forehead

JD   Vertical line through J square and below

MF   Horizontal line under M square

QF   Strong oblique mark through T of POSTAGE

PLATE 198

GG   Numerous dots in P of POSTAGE and above

TB   Diagonal line through NY of PENNY

PLATE 199

CG   Diagonal scratch from forehead to middle of N.E. square; not in imprimatur

DH   Almost circular mark below left corner of H square

HG   Re-entry in upper squares

IG   Re-entry in the upper squares, POSTAGE, and value

PLATE 200

BG Re-entry in POSTAGE and above

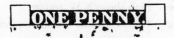

EA   Re-entry in POSTAGE and blurred marks below

FA   Blurred marks above

FD   Blurred marks below

GD   Re-entry in the upper squares, and top margin

NJ   Slight re-entry in the N.W. square, and POSTAGE

PLATE 201

AE   Left serif of A extends beyond left margin

CI   Re-entry in value

MH   Horizontal line under M square

OK   Re-entry N.E. square and value

QH   Q small and closed (see Note below)

TG   Blob in T square

TH   Blob in T square, similar to TG

Note : The letter Q is blurred throughout this plate

PLATE 203

AC   Re-entry in POSTAGE, A square, and value

DA   Re-entry in the N.W. and D squares, and POSTAGE

OA   Horizontal line under O square

TH   Re-entry POSTAGE and upper squares

Alphabet I   Alphabet II

Alphabet I   Alphabet II

Alphabet III

DIE I

[Plate 5]

DIE I

1. Stones in upper row in band appear to be round.
2. Shading below band of diadem very light.
3. Shading on upper eyelid very faint.
4. Entire nose quite straight.
5. Lower eyelid slightly shaded with dots.
6. Shading on eyeball very slight.
7. Nostril comparatively straight.
8. Mouth open, showing short upper lip.
9. Top of chin, just under lower lip, forms a curve.
10. Bottom of chin shaded with dots.
11. Top of band behind ear faint.
12. Lower edge of band formed by two faint lines, spaced.
13. Penultimate twist of pendent curl runs down towards next twist.
14. Shading on external rim of ear comparatively heavy.
15. Lobule of ear curves slightly towards front of ear.
16. Cheek very delicately shaded.

[*Plate 6*]

DIE II

1. Deep shading at side of each stone in upper row gives diamond-shaped appearance.
2. Shading below band of diadem very heavy.
3. Eight heavy lines at right angles to curve of upper eyelid.
4. Nose at juncture with forehead concave, giving bridge convex appearance.
5. Lower eyelid heavily shaded with lines.
6. Shading on eyeball very pronounced.
7. Nostril larger and distinctly arched, with heavier shading.
8. Mouth almost closed, showing much longer upper lip.
9. Top of chin shows a distinct indentation, making lower lip much fuller.
10. Line added to bottom of chin, following its curve up to indentation.
11. Top of band behind ear quite distinct.
12. Lower edge of band formed by thick line; no white space.
13. Penultimate twist of pendent curl curves round towards centre of same.
14. Shading on external rim of ear lighter and less distinct.
15. Lobule of ear ends abruptly on reaching its lowest point.
16. Shading of cheek much heavier, and of coarser character.

[Plate 7]

Alphabet II   Alphabet III

Alphabet III   Alphabet III

Alphabet IV   Alphabet IV

DIE II

[*Plate 8*]

PLATE 204

MI   Horizontal line under M square

PLATE R2

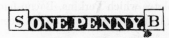

AA   Re-entry in the upper squares
      and value; coloured spots in
      the N.E. and S.E. squares

SB   Blob of colour under B square

PLATE R3

MJ   Horizontal line under M square

MK   Horizontal line under M square

PLATE R4

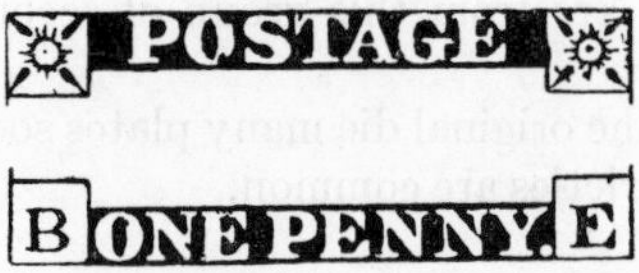

POSTAGE

B ONE PENNY E

BE   Slight re-entry in the upper
      corners and POSTAGE

RL   Circular mark on left margin

PLATE R5

MB   Horizontal line under M square

MJ   Horizontal line under M square

ND   Irregular shaped mark starting
      in D of ND and going through
      and beyond N square of NE

NE   See ND

SD   Horizontal line under S square

PLATE R6

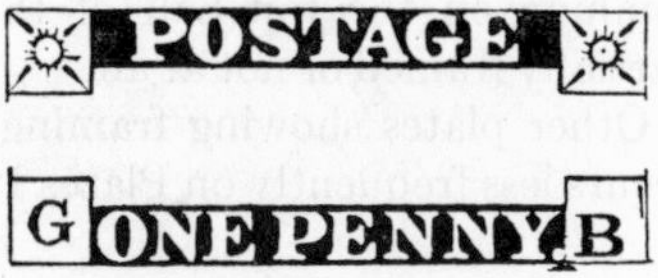

POSTAGE

GB   Horizontal mark close to B
      square

MC   Horizontal line under M square

Unplated

Note: The following four stamps
were listed by Seymour and had not
been finally identified when this
edition went to press

POSTAGE

AE   Re-entry in the upper squares
      and POSTAGE

POSTAGE

A ONE PENNY J

AJ   Striking re-entry in the N.E.
      square, a vertical line in the
      N.W. and A squares; double
      horizontal line under NY of
      PENNY and the J square

LL   Slight re-entry in the N.E.
      square

TB   Slight double impression in the
      upper squares and POSTAGE

FRAMED STAMPS

Many stamps on Plate 185 are framed on one side or both; this is more common on the top half of the sheet. The lower half shows many partially framed or not at all. Other plates showing framing on one side are 163, 194 and 197. It occurs less frequently on Plates 190, 195 and 196.

REPAIRED AND WORN PLATES

Plate 155 was put to press on November 30th, 1852, and defaced on August 28th, 1854. In Perkins, Bacon's Engraving Book there is mention of its being repaired on April 27th, 1854. There is every likelihood, therefore, that it is one of the plates which Perkins, Bacon had selected for their experiment of printing from plates which had not been hardened.*

Seymour, in the first edition, included among his illustrations six re-entries from this plate, including two states of BB. The details of these extensive repairs have been described fully, with illustrations, in the *Great Britain Philatelist*.†

Other plates found in more than one state include 173, 174, 176 (one of the plates first used for experimental printings from the unhardened state) and 178; but research into this subject is not yet sufficiently far advanced for any details to be given. It is almost certain that the unplated re-entries described on page 25 are from this group of second states.

Owing to the increasing weakness of the original die many plates soon showed signs of wear, and worn plate varieties are common.

PERFORATION 14

The 14 perforation was introduced in January 1855, just before plates from Die II were put to press, and therefore examples of Die I with this perforation are scarce. Some plates from Die I continued in use for months until they were worn, and so plates from both dies were used concurrently. Unused blocks are scarce and expensive, and corner pieces are extremely rare.

This issue presents many difficulties but as there are many fine variations of colour an attractive display of these can be formed.

---

* *The Line Engraved Postage Stamps of Great Britain*, by Sir E. D. Bacon, Vol I, p. 137.
† *Great Britain Philatelist*, Vol I, No 4, p. 67 *et seq*.

TABLES OF RARITY

The following tables show the proportionate variety of the plateable stamps of the One Penny Die I Perforated. It has been drawn up from a careful study of over 23,000 stamps.

I. Perforated 16: estimated proportion in 100,000 stamps

Plate	Total	Plate	Total	Plate	Total
155	2211	174	2076	192	1950
157	1860	175	2187	193	1986
158	0	176	5696	194	2223
159	0	177	2583	195	1436
160	6	178	2464	196	2458
161	6	179	2790	197	1696
162	1490	180	2631	198	1891
163	810	181	2406	199	886
164	1872	182	1815	200	1560
165	874	183	1867	201	1431
166	2386	184	1815	202	2057
167	2231	185	2062	203	1465
168	83	186	1413	204	874
169	1814	187	1566	R1	2175
170	501	188	2300	R2	2346
171	1832	189	1714	R3	2033
172	2646	190	1938	R4	1879
173	2953	191	2211	R5	2205
				R6	2340

II. Perforated 14: estimated proportion in 10,000 stamps

Plate	Total	Plate	Total	Plate	Total
192	12	200	259	R1	973
193	6	201	385	R2	1287
194	176	202	1127	R3	914
195	79	203	411	R4	895
196	249	204	599	R5	906
197	108			R6	1195
198	419				
199	0				

Chapter Three

Fourth Issue of One Penny Perforated

DIE II: ALPHABET II

The differences between Die I and Die II were explained by the late J. B. Seymour in Part One. For the convenience of the reader, however, facing plates have been inserted between pp. 24 and 25 showing enlarged photographs of the dies with the differences indicated, reproduced from the corresponding plates in Wright and Creeke.

PLATES 1 to 21

A new series of plate numbers began with the introduction of the retouched die. Plate 1 was registered on 15th January, 1855 and Plate 21, the last with Alphabet II, on the 8th June, 1855; thus twenty-one plates were put into use in less than five months.

The Large Crown watermark came into use in the middle of 1855 so that examples exist with both watermarks and also perforated 16 and 14 (Plates 1–15).

The papers used during this period differ considerably. A very thin greyish paper was almost certainly experimental. Very thick paper may be found which did not become so deeply blued as the normal thickness employed. Some inks caused much more blueing than others, an example being the copper colour, in which the blueing is often mottled as well. The blueing was very slight in many cases. Care must however be taken to exclude those stamps which have been subjected to chemical treatment to remove the blueing. Experienced collectors have no difficulty in rejecting these, and in nearly every case the colour of the ink is altered to give the clue.

Transitional shades on toned paper, mentioned later, are very rare, and only occur because the plates in question were still in use in 1857.

These plates were not laid down very accurately; consequently the number of off-centre specimens is proportionally very large. Being in use for a short time they are thus not very common and are really scarce in fine, well-centred condition.

A collection of nicely centred plated copies of the various shades, watermarks and perforations makes a very attractive display, and is

28

PLATE 1   29

probably more pleasing to the eye than stamps from any other period of the Penny red issue.

Printings from these plates appear in early April 1855 and continue until April to May, 1856. They overlap therefore with the earliest plates of Alphabet III; Plates 22 onwards. Dated pieces being scarce, sufficient evidence is not available to give a reliable guide to the earliest and latest dates recorded of the individual plates.

PLATE 1

Summary. Put to press 16.1.1855; defaced 8.5.1856; sheets printed not known, but estimated at 120,000; Alphabet II check letters; Imprimatur sheet in chocolate-brown on markedly blued paper watermarked small crown.

Colour. The majority of the printings were in a light red-brown colour on slightly blued paper. Darker brown colours do occur occasionally on very blue paper, whilst very rarely printings were made in a copper-brown colour on blue paper.

Perforation, 16 and 14; *Watermark,* Small and Large Crown. All combinations are known and the proportions work out at SC 16, 34%; SC 14, 24%; LC 16, 5%; LC 14, 37%.

Check letters. These are almost always low in the squares; there are a few exceptions and those markedly differing from this rule are illustrated. P is blind throughout save for PD, PI, PJ which have an open loop. For these a different punch was used, the P being slightly taller. S is thin lined.

Notes. The alignment of the plate is fairly accurate but is generally slightly narrow between the vertical J and K rows. QJ and QK are extremely close together.

A mint half sheet is known, also a few smaller pieces. Off-centre is common.

AG   Spot on tip of bust

AK   K double

AL   Large dot below upright of L, possibly trace of double letter

BG   Different punch used for G; G with defective shortened serif to right

CL   Large dot almost touches right margin two-thirds way down

DA   Spot behind corner of mouth

EH   H lightly struck

FB   Defective impression in S.E. square

FF   Bottom line extends on right

FH   Different punch for H used; H larger than normal

HH   Large dot beneath lower right serif of second H touching base line

IG
JG   Different punch used for G; G with defective shortened serif to right; see BG
KG
LG

JI   Right side of horizontal bar of T partially blotted out

LA   Large dot to top of right of L

LD   Lower serif of D lengthened

MD   Spot on nose

MG   Vee of M extends downwards as a thin line

MH   Horizontal line beneath M square; mark in top left side of O of ONE; indefinite marks on base of G

ML   Vee of M extends downwards as thin line

ND   Letter D lightly struck

NE   Base of E extends backwards as a fine line

OF   Letter O lightly struck

OJ   Misplaced letters

PG   Bottom line extends on right

PJ   Letter P not blind

QA   Base of Q faint

QB   Large dot in top of B

QE   Blur over lower half of Q

QH   Different punch used for Q; Q larger than normal

PLATE 1   31

RG   Top of G double

QI   Spot on cheek behind mouth   RI   Misplaced letters

QJ   Misplaced letters

SC   Short scratch in margin be-
       tween SC and SD on level
       with tip of bust

TA   Lower right serif of A extends
       to right

RD   Mark in upper half of right
       side of O of POSTAGE

PLATE 2

Summary. Put to press 20.1.1855; defaced 8.5.1856; sheets printed not known, but estimated at 120,000; Alphabet II check letters; Imprimatur sheet in chestnut-brown on very markedly blued paper watermarked small crown.

Colour. The majority of the printings were in a light red-brown colour on slightly blued paper. Very rarely a coppery colour may be found on deeply blued paper.

Perforation, 16 and 14; *Watermark,* Small and Large Crown. All combinations are known and the proportions work out at SC 16, 40%; SC 14, 28%; LC 16, 2%; LC 14, 30%.

Check letters. These are almost always low in their squares; there are a few exceptions and those markedly differing to this rule are illustrated. P is blind throughout except for PL which has an open loop.

Notes. The alignment is not very uniform, the spacing being fairly wide between the vertical A, B and C rows causing the spacing between H-L vertical rows to become congested. Many impressions are very close together whilst QF-QG, RF-RG, SF-SG, TF-TG are almost touching each other.

No important mint pieces are known; off-centre is common.

AH   Short gash and spot on chin

BF   Large spot on nose

BI   Large spot above B and vertical line in N.E. square; possibly re-entry

CE   Large dot in top of N.W. square

CI   Large dot in centre of T

CK   Lower right serif of K extended through side of square; K far to right

EC   Misplaced letters

EE   Misplaced letters

EG   Different punch for E used; E larger than normal

FG   Spot on collar bone

GE   Coloured mark on left side extending slightly into margin opposite chin

HA   Right side extends above

HE   Very slight prolongation downwards of left side of H

HF   Small scratch above N.E. major ray in N.E. square

IA   Large circular mark on hair above lower curl

IB   Dot outside N.E. corner

IC   Left side extends above

JG   Spot beneath ear

KB   Lower serif of B extends to left as thin line

LA   Large dot in margin well below S.E. corner

MA   Large dot in margin above corner of N.E. square (see LA); bottom line extends slightly on right

NC   Left side extends above

NG   Different punch used; G larger than normal

OG   Slight burr rub in POSTAGE

PLATE 2   33

PH   Thin vertical line connects left
      leg of H to base line

PL   Different punch used; P open
      and slightly taller

QI   Large mark on brow

QB   Large spot in margin over T of
      POSTAGE

RB   Mark on eyebrow

QE   Blur over lower half of Q

RE   Top line extends on left

QF   Vertical mark in margin below
      P of PENNY

SL   Misplaced letters

PLATE 3

Summary. Put to press 22.1.1855; defaced 8.5.1856; sheets printed not
known but estimated at 34,000; Alphabet II check letters; Imprimatur
sheet in red-brown on slightly blued paper watermarked small crown.

Colour. The majority of the printings were in a light red-brown colour on
slightly blued paper. Darker red-brown shades on deeply blue paper
occur rarely.

Perforation, 16 and 14; *Watermark,* Small and Large Crown. Only three
combinations are known to date, and even LC 14 is scarce: SC 16, 34%;
SC 14, 58%; LC 16, 0%; LC 14, 8%.

Check letters. These are almost always low in their squares. There are a
few exceptions and those markedly differing to this rule are illustrated.
P is blind throughout.

Notes. The alignment is not very uniform. The A, B, C rows tend to be
widely spaced and the I, J, K, L rows more closely spaced. SD-SE, TD-TE,
SH-SI, TH-TI are very close together.

   No mint pieces are known. The plate is rather rare and many copies
are badly off-centre.

AE   Scratch on tip of bust

DE   Dot below S.W. corner of E
      square

EL   Misplaced letters

C

GE   Top line extends on right

GI   Irregular marks on GE, nearly obliterating both letters

GL   Large spot behind nose

HG   Marks in O and top of N of ONE

IA   Coincident re-entry; both letters faint

IB   Different punch used; letter B larger than normal

IF   Large dot in left side of O of ONE

KI   Right side extends above

LA   Coincident re-entry; both letters faint

LC   Faint line attaches lower left serif of L to base of square; marked burr line in both side margins

ND   Vertical line close to upright of D square

NI   Marks in margin between   NE
OI   OS

OE   Large blob attached to N.E. major ray in N.W. square

OF   Spot on base of neck

PE   Different punch for E used; E larger than normal

PG   Small scratch above eye

QB   B slightly double above

QE   Different punch for E used; E larger than normal

QK   Coincident re-entry; both letters faint and burr line left margin

RB   Coloured margin in right margin two-thirds way down; lower portion of B defective

RG   Coincident re-entry; both letters faint; burr line extending entire length of left side and three-quarters length of right side from top

SD   Mark on left side opposite mouth

SH   Crossbar of H faint

SI   Misplaced letters

PLATE 4   35

PLATE 4

Summary. Put to press 20.1.1855; defaced 8.5.1856; sheets printed not known, but estimated at 130,000; Alphabet II check letters; Imprimatur sheet in brown on slightly blued paper watermarked small crown.

Colour. The majority of the printings were in a light red-brown colour on slightly blued paper. Deep chocolate colours may be found on deeply blued paper and the coppery brown shade may also be seen.

Perforation, 16 and 14; *Watermark,* Small and Large Crown. All combinations occur and the proportion works out at SC 16, 26%; SC 14, 22%; LC 16, 3%; LC 14, 49%.

Check letters. These are almost always low in their squares; there are a few exceptions and those markedly differing from this rule are illustrated. P is blind throughout.

Notes. The alignment is quite good. The spacing between the E and F vertical rows is somewhat wide and that between the H and I vertical rows is narrow. TH-TI are very close together.

A few small mint pieces are known. Printings from this plate seem to occur more often than from any other plate of this group. Off-centre copies are common.

BC	Horizontal scratch through Y and C square near base line (see BD)	FE	Top line extends slightly on right

BD Horizontal scratch through ONE P near base line (see BC)

BL Thin horizontal scratch connects toe of L to right side of square

FI Several dots round corner of mouth

DD Top line extends on right

EA Tiny dot close to N.E. corner of N.E. square

GH Misplaced letters

HA A double

HE Top line extends on right

EJ Misplaced letters

HF Bottom line extends on right

IL   Large spot on left margin above I square, partly on lateral network in left margin

JC   Bottom line extends on right

JH   Short horizontal line below S.W. corner of H square

JI   Different punch for J used; ball well curved

LD   Lower loop of D broken

MB   Top line extends slightly on right

OA   Mark after top of A except on early prints

RA   Bottom line weak below E PE

RB   Dot in top of upright of P of PENNY

RE   Bottom line weak below E PE

RG   Bottom line extends slightly on right

ONE PENNY.

ONE PENNY.

RK   Fresh entry in value (normal above)

SC   Dot on margin above P and spot on bust near tip

SF   Bottom line extends on right

SG   Misplaced letters

SL   Margin weak over E

TB   Bottom line extends on right

PLATE 5

Summary. Put to press 3.2.1855; defaced 8.5.1856; sheets printed not known, but estimated at 120,000; Alphabet II check letters; Imprimatur sheet in red-brown on slightly blued paper watermarked small crown.

Colour. The majority of the printings were in a red-brown colour on slightly blued paper. Darker shades occur and occasionally a copper colour on deeply blued paper is seen.

Perforation, 16 and 14; *Watermark,* Small and Large Crown. All combinations occur and the proportion works out at SC 16, 36%; SC 14, 24%; LC 16, 2%; LC 14, 38%.

Check letters. This plate has the well known small G, which occurs on all

PLATE 5   37

stamps in the vertical G rows except FG, HG, MG, and in the horizontal rows except GC, GE, GG (first G), GH. A different punch was used for these and it appears on Plate 6. The majority of the check letters on this plate have the letters placed fairly high in the squares, but some are very low and have been illustrated.

The S is inverted on SD to SL and has been made with a different punch to that used for SA, SB and SC. The S for the latter is thin lined and the inverted S has a thicker central portion and resembles that used for Plate 4. It is possible that the S was incorrectly inserted in the holder but there is no proof of this. A mistake is more likely to be the cause. The thin-lined S used for SA, SB, SC was used for the S row on Plate 6.

Notes. The alignment is quite good save for the vertical J row which is placed too close to the I row throughout its length. DI-DJ, II-IJ, OI-OJ, are extremely close together.

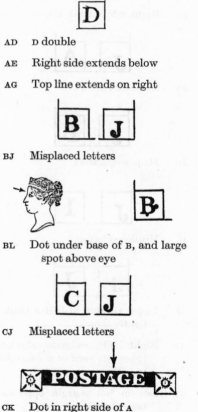

AD   D double

AE   Right side extends below

AG   Top line extends on right

BJ   Misplaced letters

BL   Dot under base of B, and large spot above eye

CJ   Misplaced letters

CK   Dot in right side of A

CL   Large blot in top of O of POSTAGE extending into margin above; misplaced letters

DJ   Misplaced letters

DL   Dot in margin above S

EA   Lower left serif of A extends to touch side of square

EB   Bottom line extends on right

EG   G square recut

EK   Dot to left of top of upper left serif of K which just touches side line

FA   Misplaced letters

FB   Top line extends very slightly on right

FG   Evidence of double G seen on early deep printings; original G was extremely high, touching top of square

FH   Large blob in lateral network above F square

FJ   Mark on top of ear

FK   Large spot on brow; dot very near N.W. corner of N.E. square in upper segment

FL   Lower third of left side recut with F square out of true on left side; base line shortened; F extremely close to right and high; large dot in upright of P of POSTAGE opposite loop

GA   Bottom line extends slightly on right and left

GB   Big dot within letter G

GG   Dot in upper portion of second letter G

GI   Dot within letter G

GK   Large dot in upper curve of S

HB   B double

IC   Bottom line extends on right; misplaced letters

IK   Right side extends above

JA   Misplaced letters

JD   Misplaced letters

JI   Misplaced letters

JJ   Upper portion of first J faint, lightly struck

KH   Right side extends above; lower left serif of H extends to left

KI   Dot in left margin opposite base of neck

PLATE 5   39

LF   Misplaced letters

LJ   Fresh entry POSTAGE, value and letter squares

LK   Different punch for L used; L thinner and slightly larger.

LL   Large dot and blur mark above first L

MA   Large dot in centre of upright of P of PENNY

MG   Very large dot attached to S.W. corner of M square

MI   Large dot attached to S.W. corner of M square

MJ   Marked fresh entry upper squares, POSTAGE, value and in margin below

NE   Different punch used; E larger than normal

NL   Dot in base of loop of P of PENNY

OJ   Upper two-thirds of left side absent; lower third is present and has been markedly strengthened

PB   }   Different punch used for P; P
PF   }   larger and more clearly formed

QB   Bottom line extends on left

RA   Tiny dot below and attached to oblique stroke of N of ONE; coloured mark in right lateral network nearly half way down

RB   Dot attached to loop of R

RC   Misplaced letters

RG   R double

SA   Mark in margin over O of POSTAGE

SB   Large dot in centre of oblique stroke on N of ONE

SD   s inverted

SE   s inverted

SF   s inverted

SG   s inverted

SH   s inverted

SI   s inverted

SJ   s inverted

SK   s inverted

SL   s inverted

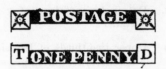

TD   Fresh entry POSTAGE and value

TG   Marks within letter G

TI   Short line below S.W. corner of I square

TJ   Bottom line extends on left

TK   Bottom line extends on left

PLATE 6

Summary. Put to press 3.2.1855; defaced 8.5.1856; sheets printed not known, but estimated at 120,000; Alphabet II check letters; Imprimatur sheet is in red-brown on slightly blued paper watermarked small crown.

Colour. The majority of the printings were in a red-brown colour on blue paper. Darker shades occur and occasionally a copper colour on deeply blued paper is seen.

Perforation, 16 and 14; *Watermark,* Small and Large Crown. All combinations occur and the proportion works out at SC 16, 29%; SC 14, 25%; LC 16, 4%; LC 14, 42%.

Check letters. A few small G's, such as occur on Plate 5, also appear on this plate. They are: BG, EG, HG, LG, MG, NG, GC, GE, GI, GJ. The letters are nearly all placed high in their squares but exceptions occur when they are low and extreme cases are illustrated. The margins of the letter squares have been damaged in a number of instances by inaccurate punching, e.g. DL, EL, HL, IK, IL, QB. The S is moderately tall, thin-lined, and was used for SA, SB and SC of Plate 5; it was not used on any other plate.

Notes. The alignment is good. TD-TE are rather close together.

AI   Top and bottom left serifs of I defective

AL   L extremely far to right side of square and side of this square is missing opposite toe of L

BB   Different punch used for B; both B's larger than normal

BJ   Mark in right side of O of POSTAGE, not in early copies

CI   Short vertical mark attached to base of C square

DA   Vertical thin line parallel and close to left side of D square; vertical line in N.E. square close to frame

DD   Horizontal scratch in top of first D square and horizontal scratch below first D square

DG   Tiny dot in S.W. corner of G square

DL   D extremely low central and base of D square defective

PLATE 6   41

EG   Dot in S.W. corner of G square;
      different punch used for E;
      E larger than normal

EH   Fresh entry upper squares and
      POSTAGE

EL   Right side of L square defec-
      tive

FB   Large mark to left of F

FG   Dot attached to outside of
      S.W. corner of G square

FI   Base line of I square weak
      below I, which is low central

FK   Right side of K square weak in
      centre

FL   Right side of L square missing
      opposite toe of L

GE   Dot in top of letter G

GG   Second G defective with right
      half recut and the right half
      of horizontal serif of this G is
      missing

HG   Large dot within G and dot in
      S.W. corner of G square

HL   Right side of L square defec-
      tive

IB   Right side extends above

ID   Small dot in front of D

IH   Dot in S.W. corner of H square

IK   Base of I square weak in
      centre

L

IL   L extremely high and very far
      to right; right side of L
      square defective

JB   Vertical stroke in front of B,
      possibly evidence of double
      B; different punch used for
      B; B larger than normal

JH   Dot within H square near S.W.
      corner touching base line

JI   Tiny dot to left of and slightly
      above top left serif of I

KA   Dot in slant of N of ONE near
      top

KB   Different punch used for B;
      B larger than normal

KF   Large dot in S.W. corner of F
      square

KG   Large dot below S.W. corner of
      G square

KH   Dot in S.W. corner of H square

LC   Blur in top of T

LE   Base of L square weak

LF   Blot in base of P and blot in left side of O of POSTAGE in late state

LH   Dot in S.W. corner of H square

LJ   Tiny short stroke in extreme N.W. corner of L square

LK   Tiny dot beneath E of ONE

LL   Base of first L square weak in centre, and right side of second L square weak in centre of lower third

MF   Dot in S.W. corner of M square

MH   Dot in S.W. corner of H square

NI   Dot in N.E. corner of N square, not seen in early copies

OE   Large dot below S.W. corner of O square

OF   Large dot between base of F and S.W. corner of F square

OG   Large dot below S.W. corner of G square

PB   Different punch used for P; P taller than normal

PF   Tiny dot in S.W. corner of F square

PK   Different punch used for P; P with larger loop than normal

QA   Top of Q faint

QB   Large break in right side of B square

QD   Break in base of D

QE   Two large dots in left foot of A and one dot in right foot of A; dot below right upright of second N of PENNY

RB   Mark obscuring upper and inner aspect of left side of O of POSTAGE

RG   Tiny scratch below S.W. corner of G square

SB   Different punch used for B; B larger than normal

SG   Dot below S.W. corner of G square

TH   Dot outside S.W. corner of H square

TJ   Top line of T square irregular

TA–TL   T is taller than in preceding plates

PLATE 7

Summary. Put to press 7.2.1855; defaced 8.5.1856; sheets printed not known, but estimated at 90,000; Alphabet II check letters; Imprimatur sheet in red-brown on slightly blued paper watermarked small crown.

Colour. The majority of the printings were in a red-brown colour on blue

PLATE 7 43

paper. Deeper shades occur and a copper colour occasionally is seen on very blue paper.

Perforation, 16 and 14; *Watermark*, Small and Large Crown. All combinations occur and the proportion works out at SC 16, 17%; SC 14, 20%; LC 16, 4%; LC 14, 59%.

Check letters. The general arrangement of check letters occurring on Plates 1–6 ceases with this plate; the position of the check letters does not follow a set pattern. The base of B curves inwards except on QB, SB and TB.

Notes. The alignment is good, but the D and E vertical rows are somewhat close. TD-TE are very close.

The plate suffered from corrosion; a number of marks due to this cause are found spread uniformly over the surface.

AE   Large dot in right side of O of ONE near base

AI   Tiny dot below S.W. corner of A square

AK   Dot to left of foot of A and dot attached to right serif of A

BH   Smudged dot outside corner of N.E. square

BI   Dot in base of T and dot in centre of N.E. square

DJ   D retouched and flattened

EB   Scratch attached to lower loop of B

EC   Large spot on tip of bust (see FC)

EG   Dot outside S.W. corner of G square

EL   Dot attached to outside of N.W. corner of E square

FA   Short vertical stroke very close to and to the left of upright of F

FC   Spot on tip of bust (see EC)

FF   Large dot in margin a short way below N.E. square, and dot in base of S

FG   Big spot beneath eye

ONE PENNY.

FI	Large dot in P of PENNY
GB	Dot below S.W. corner of B square
GD	Dot in bottom margin well below NY (see HD)
GI	Dot in middle of upright of E of PENNY
HD	Dot in top margin well above E of POSTAGE (see GD)
HI	Dot in margin over TA
HK	Very large dot below centre of base line of H square

POSTAGE

IB	Indentation into top of loop of P of POSTAGE
IC	Lateral network very worn opposite back of neck

IL	Misplaced letters

JA	Dot in front of J

JB	Short horizontal stroke attached to left side of B square and in close proximity to top left serif of B; spot on shoulder

JG	Large spot on top of letter G
JH	Bottom line extends slightly on right

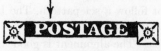

POSTAGE

KB	Large spot on shoulder; another on neck; large blot in left side of O of POSTAGE
KI	Dot attached to base of K square below right foot

LB	Large spot below corner of mouth
LK	Blur within top of K

MB	Lower right serif of M connected by fine scratch to right side of square; dot below S.W. corner of B square and dot in corner of B square; dot below upright of B

MF	Triangular mark above ear (see NF)

PLATE 7   45

NA   Top line extends slightly on right

NC   Dot beneath C

NF   Triangular mark above ear (see MF)

NG   Dot below S.W. corner of N square

OC   Large spot below ear

OG   Large dot in N.E. corner of G square

PB   Lower loop of B faint

QB   Different punch for B used; B with flat base

QD   Big dot in lower margin below foot of second N close to frame

QE   Big dot in lower margin below foot of second N not close to frame

QI   Bottom line extends on left

RA   Spot on cheek between base of ear and corner of mouth

RD   Tiny dot below S.W. corner of R square and short vertical scratch on side of neck

RE   E recut and much enlarged; large dot in margin above, approximately half way between GE and second N of PENNY

RK   Different punch used for R; R with larger loop

SB   Large smudge on S.W. corner of S square; large dot below and close to E of ONE; B with flat base

SF   Large dot below ear

POSTAGE

SG   Large blot obscuring majority of upper half of T

TB   Dot in right margin above B; B with flat base

PLATE 8

Summary. Put to press 24.3.55; defaced 8.5.56; sheets printed not known, but estimated at 90,000; Alphabet II check letters; Imprimatur sheet in red-brown on slightly blued paper watermarked small crown.

Colour. The majority of the printings were in red-brown on blue paper. The red-brown varies in depth. Very deep copper colour shades occur occasionally on deeply blued paper.

Perforation, 16 and 14; *Watermark*, Small and Large Crown. All combinations are known and the proportion works out at SC 16, 20%; SC 14, 22%; LC 16, 2%; LC 14, 56%.

Check letters. Two punches were used for letter E. The middle bar is central on EA, EE, EJ and placed slightly higher on all the remainder. The letters were placed fairly accurately in their squares.

Notes. The alignment of this plate is quite accurate; the only notable exception is that TC TD are rather close together.

No fresh entries have been found. A block of sixty mint stamps is known.

AI Large spot on neck

BH Large dot in top of E of ONE; dot above upright of B

CG Blurred dot in N.W. corner of G square

CI Spot on upper part of throat

FC Dot in F square to right of top right serif of F almost touches right side of square

HK Dot in upper half of H

IK Short blurred vertical stroke in front of I

JD Dot above J nearly touches top of square

JG Dot outside S.W. corner of G square

JI Short vertical stroke in front of J and dot after J close to right side of square

LC Blur in top of A (see MC and NC) and large dot in top of lower curve of G

LD Curved mark in front of L

MC Blur in top of A (see LC and NC)

NC Blur in top of A (see LC and MC); top line extends slightly on right

NG Dot below ear

PLATE 8   47

NJ   Dot in N.W. corner of J square

OB   Large dot in upper right fork
      of Y

OE   Large dot attached to top line
      near top right corner of E of
      POSTAGE

OJ   Dot and heavy blur in front
      of top of J

PC   Large dot in base of P of
      POSTAGE

QB   Large dot attached to base of
      B square

QC   Dot on top of head
SC   Dot in lower part of C
SI   Dot to left of top of I
SJ   Tiny dot outside S.W. corner
      of S square
TG   Marks within letter G and dot
      S.W. corner of T square

TI   Several dots on bust

PLATE 9

Summary. Put to press 24.3.55; defaced 8.5.56; sheets printed not known but estimated at 100,000; Alphabet II check letters; Imprimatur sheet in red-brown on slightly blued paper watermarked small crown.

Colour. The majority of the printings were in red-brown on blued paper. The depth of red-brown varies.

Perforation, 16 and 14; *Watermark,* Small and Large Crown. All combinations are known and the proportion works out at SC 16, 20%; SC 14, 24%; LC 16, 55%; LC 14, 1%.

Re-entry. There is a re-entry, very nearly coincident, on IG which has caused considerable compression on the check letters, which consequently appear faint. POSTAGE and ONE PENNY also appear contracted. There is a trace of the former in the upper major rays of the N.W. and N.E. squares. This subsequent entry has been placed slightly to the right (as it appears on the printed stamp).

Check letters. These were placed fairly accurately in their squares.

Note. The alignment of this plate is not very accurate. Many stamps are placed close together.

AB   Vertical thin line connects left serif of A to base line

AL   L double

BC   Dot below S.W. corner of B square

BJ   Dot below S.W. corner of B square

CJ   Dot over os close to frame

CL   Short horizontal scratch above top right serif of L

DC   Two dots within c, scarcely visible in late printings

DD   Dot below S.W. corner of second D square

ED   Tiny dot to right of top right serif of E almost touches right side of square

EG   Dot below S.W. corner of G square

FB   Dot below S.W. corner of B square

FC   Large spot on centre of cheek

FF   Thick vertical mark above top left corner of first F, tapering to thin line which extends to left side of square

GG   Dot below S.W. corner of second G square

GH   Dot below S.W. corner of G square

HD   Horizontal scratch beneath right half of base line of H square

HG   Dot within base of letter G

HI   Tiny dot within upper arms of H

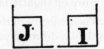

IG   Coincident re-entry; both letters faint and POSTAGE and value are slightly smaller in size

II   Short blurred vertical stroke in front of second I

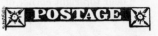

JH   Dot in front of J

JI   Dot after top of J and tiny dot in N.W. corner of I square

KC   Dot below S.W. corner of K square

KJ   Dot below S.W. corner of K square

MA   Large dot in top left corner of E of POSTAGE

PLATE 9   49

MD   Different punch for D used; D larger than normal

M-E   N-E

ME   Spot on ear

NB   Dot below S.W. corner of B square

NE   Spot on ear; see ME

OG   Large dot below S.W. corner of G square; right side extends slightly above

PC   Right side extends very slightly above

PL   P double

QJ   Dot in N.W. corner of J square

RD   Tiny dot below S.W. corner of R square

SA   Dot below S.W. corner of A square

TA   Dot below S.W. corner of A square

TE   Tiny dot below S.W. corner of T and E squares

TG   Dot below S.W. corner of T square, and large spot in centre of oblique bar of N of ONE

TJ   Dot below S.W. corner of T square; bottom line extends slightly on right

TK   Dot below S.W. corner of K square and heavy mark on right network nearly half way down

TL   Dot close to right margin two-thirds way down

PLATE 10

Summary. Put to press 11.4.55; defaced 8.5.56; sheets printed not known but estimated at 80,000; Alphabet II check letters; Imprimatur sheet in red-brown on slightly blued paper watermarked small crown.

Colour. The majority of printings are in red-brown on blued paper. The depth varies but deep red-brown and a copper-brown on deeply blued paper may be seen.

Perforation, 16 and 14; *Watermark,* Small and Large Crown. All combinations are known and the proportion works out at SC 16, 17%; SC 14, 24%; LC 16, 2%; LC 14, 57%.

Fresh entries. These occur on KK, KL and QE. KK was originally placed slightly too low. KL was far too high and considerable marks remain in the top margin of the former entry. QE was originally slightly too far to

D

right (as it appears on the stamp). Both letters have been recut by hand and the characteristic appearance thus lost.

Check letters. These are fairly accurately placed in their squares.

Notes. The alignment of this plate is only moderately accurate. The vertical K and L rows are rather close together; IK, JA, JL and MC are placed far too high.

AK   Large spot on top of T

BD   Dot in front of D

CJ   Dot in lower part of C

CL   Burr rub POSTAGE

DL   Burr rub TAGE

EG   Tiny dot outside S.W. corner of G square

EL   Burr rub TAGE

GC   Dot in upper part of letter G

GG   Dot in upper portions of both letters G

HA   Dot below S.W. corner of A square

HH   Second H double at top

IJ   Blurred short stroke in front of top of J

IK   Entry placed far too high

JA   Entry placed far too high

JB   Dot outside S.W. corner of B square

JG   Dot below S.W. corner of G square

JH   Spot on ear

JL   Entry placed far too high

KK   Fresh entry, chiefly in N.E. square and second K square

KL   Marked fresh entry, all squares, POSTAGE, value and top margin

LA   Small mark in margin below left leg of second N of PENNY

LJ   Large spot in front of top serif of J

LK   Dot below S.W. corner of L and K squares

MC   Entry placed far too high

NH   H lightly struck and appears very faint

PLATE 10   51

NL   Spot below and to right of base of neck; large dot in margin below E of PENNY

OF   Dot between TA near top line

OI   Dot below S.W. corner of I square

OJ   Dot below S.W. corner of O square

PB   Dot almost touching base line below serif of P

PD   Four marks on shoulder

PI   Dot outside corner of P square

QE   Fresh entry, not very evident; mark in margin below E square; both letters have been recut by hand

RA   Horizontal bar of A extremely weak and absent in later printings

RB   Mark between loop of R and side of square

RF   Tiny dot attached to S.W. corner of R square

RI   Large dot in top of R square

SK   Large dot outside S.W. corner of K square

TG   Dot outside S.W. corner of T square and short vertical scratch on collar bone

TI   Dot below S.E. corner of T square

TK   Large spot at base of neck anteriorly

PLATE 11

Summary. Put to press 16.4.1855; defaced 8.5.1856; sheets printed not known, but estimated at 80,000; Alphabet II check letters; Imprimatur sheet in red-brown on slightly blued paper watermarked small crown.

Colour. The majority of the printings were in red-brown on blued paper. Darker shades do occur and a chocolate colour appears occasionally. A copper colour on deeply blued paper is rarely seen.

Perforation, 16 and 14; *Watermark,* Small and Large Crown. All combinations are known and the proportion works out at SC 16, 14%; SC 14, 16%; LC 16, 5%; LC 14, 65%.

Check letters. These are moderately accurately placed in their squares.

Notes. The alignment of the plate is fairly accurate but wide and narrow spacings do occur at irregular intervals. There is the usual tendency for a general rise from left to right.

The plate is almost entirely free from any noticeable varieties and no re-entering has been discovered.

AC	Large dot immediately below central dot in N.W. square		

AJ	Dot in lower part of curve of G	NB	Dot in top margin between AG
FH	Side lines of F square cross minutely	SG	Tiny dots below S.W. corner of S and G squares
		TC	Dot below S.W. corner of T square
GK	Tiny scratch in top of letter G	TD	Dot below S.W. corner of T square
HB	B lightly struck		
HI	Crossbar of H weak		

HK	Tiny dot below S.W. corner of K square	TE	Dot below S.W. corner of T square and dot attached to left side of T square
KB	Letter B lightly struck		

PLATE 12

Summary. Put to press 19.4.1855; defaced 8.5.1856; sheets printed not known, but estimated at 80,000; Alphabet II check letters; Imprimatur sheet in a rich red-brown shade on markedly blued paper watermarked small crown.

Colour. The majority of the printings were in red-brown on blued paper. Deeper shades occur; also a chocolate shade appeared occasionally. A copper colour on deeply blued paper may also be seen, but rarely.

Perforation, 16 and 14; *Watermark,* Small and Large Crown. All

PLATE 12   53

combinations are known and the proportion works out at SC 16, 16%; SC 14, 20%; LC 16, 2%; LC 14, 62%.

Check letters. These are reasonably accurately placed.

Notes. The alignment of the plate is moderately accurate but has the usual tendency to rise from left to right. TB, TC, TD are placed very close together. No re-entering has been discovered.

BA   Big dot below S.W. corner of A square

BC   Thick vertical line extends upwards from A of POSTAGE

CK   Dot below S.W. corner of K square

DG   Mark in upper portion of loop of P of POSTAGE

II   Large spot on back of ear

KI   Dot in S.W. corner of K square

KK   Large dot in S.E. corner of first K square

LJ   Large dot in margin above E

DK   Blur on top of K

LK   Dot below S.W. corner of K square

DL   Spot to right of nostril and larger spot on cheek

MJ   Two dots vertically above foot of J

FK   Dot in S.W. corner of K square

FL   Dot below S.W. corner of L square

GL   Dot below S.W. corner of L square

NH   Tiny dot to left of lower left serif of N and vertical scratch through base line of N square

HB   Horizontal scratch in margin above STA

HI   Small dot attached to base of left upright of H

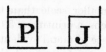

PJ   Loop of P enlarged and J is square footed, both letters being handcut

IE   Dot to left of top left serif of E

QA   Large dot almost touching top of Q square near N.E. corner

QJ   Top line of N.E. square weak; dot near N.W. corner of J square

SG   Tiny dot below S.W. corner of s square

TC   Dot over o of POSTAGE

TL   Large dot below S.W. corner of T square

PLATE 13

Summary. Put to press 23.4.1855; defaced 8.5.1856; sheets printed not known, but estimated at 50,000; Alphabet II check letters; Imprimatur sheet in rich red-brown on slightly blued paper watermarked small crown.

Colour. The majority of the printings were in red-brown on blued paper. Darker shades occur more frequently on this plate, especially the chocolate shade. Copper colour on deeply blued paper is seen.

Perforation, 16 and 14; *Watermark,* Small and Large Crown. All combinations are known and the proportion works out at SC 16, 5%; SC 14, 16%; LC 16, 2%; LC 14, 77%.

Check letters. These are placed fairly accurately in their squares.

Fresh entries. The original entry of QL was placed far too high and was corrected, POSTAGE being nearly legible in the margin between PL and QL. This is the best marked fresh entry in this group. QE also shows evidence of previous entry.

Notes. The alignment of the plate is not very accurate, narrow and wide spacings occur repeatedly. This caused a letter to be written by Ormond Hill to Perkins, Bacon on 18th May, 1855 calling attention to the irregular way the plates were being laid down, specifying Plate 13 in particular. The main defect was the irregular placing of BG, which was far too high and very close to AG. Perkins, Bacon undertook to remedy this defect if possible.*

As no repaired state of either AG or BG has been found a repair is presumed not to have been made. Printing was evidently resumed but on a smaller scale than the previous plates. From the frequency of specimens, a printing of 50,000 sheets is likely.

A piece of metal evidently became attached to the transfer roller, for a similar mark occurs on the lower right major ray in the N.E. square of AI, AJ, BI, BJ, and CJ.

---

* *Line-Engraved Postage Stamps of Great Britain,* by Sir E. D. Bacon, p. 145.

PLATE 13   55

AF	A double	MF	Vertical scratch in right side of F square touching top of square
AI	Lower right major ray in N.E. square smudged		
AJ	Lower right major ray in N.E. square smudged	MK	Dot in S.W. corner of M square
		ML	Dot below S.W. corner of L square
AK	Dot below S.W. corner of A square		
BF	Dot in S.W. corner of F square	NC	Upper right portion of N blurred
BG	Impression placed far too high	NJ	Dot in N.W. corner of J square
BI	Lower right major ray in N.E. square smudged	OK	Large dot below lower left serif of K
BJ	Lower right major ray in N.E. square smudged		
BL	Burr rub POSTAGE		

QE Evidence of fresh entry in value

CJ	Lower right major ray in N.E. square smudged, and large spot on neck	PL–QL	Very marked evidence of misplaced entry between these stamps
		QG	Dot in N.W. corner of G square
DK	Dot below S.W. corner of K square	RH	Blurred mark to left of H
DL	Burr rub POSTAGE		
FK	Dot below S.W. corner of K square		

		RL	Dot within L
KK	Tiny dot below S.W. corner of second K square	TJ	Dot below S.W. corner of T square

PLATE 14

Summary. Put to press 22.5.1855; defaced 8.5.1856; sheets printed not known, but estimated at 90,000; Alphabet II check letters; Imprimatur sheet in red-brown on slightly blued paper watermarked small crown.

Colour. The majority of the printings were in red-brown on blued paper. Deeper shades occur more frequently on this plate and copper colour on deeply blued paper may be seen.

Perforation, 16 and 14; *Watermark,* Small and Large Crown. All combinations are known and the proportion works out at SC 16, 8%; SC 14, 15%; LC 16, 3%; LC 14, 74%.

Fresh entry. TD is well marked and OE is possibly a fresh entry. There is a marked burr rub in value of NE and of POSTAGE in PE. OE shows a few marks in the value only. There is also a conspicuous mark in the upper margin between E and N.E. square of OE.

Check letters. These are moderately accurately placed in their squares.

Note. The alignment of the plate shows a considerable improvement on its predecessors. Narrow and wide spacing does occur, TH TI being very close together.

AB	Short horizontal line attached to base of lower loop of B

B-A

C-A

BA	Thick horizontal scratch under first N of PENNY
CA	One short thick and one short thin horizontal mark above AG; see BA
CG	Dot within C
CL	Dot below lower right serif of L
EH	Bottom line extends on left
FB	Dot in margin midway between FB and GB and vertically below S.W. corner of B square
FC	Dot in upper right side of O of POSTAGE
FD	Dot below S.W. corner of F square
HG	Dot near N.W. corner of G square

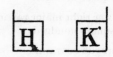

HK	Blurred mark below lower right serif of H; large dot to right of upper right serif of K
LD	Dot below S.W. corner of L square
MC	Large dot in S.W. corner of M square
MD	Top line extends slightly on right
MK	Dot below S.W. corner of K square
NB	Blur on upper half of letter N

NE	Large mark in margin below Y; burr rub PENNY

OE	Possibly a re-entry with a few marks in value
OK	Large dot above upper right serif of K
PE	Burr rub POSTAGE

PLATE 14   57

PK   Dot below S.W. corner of K square

QG   Dot below S.W. corner of G square

QI   Dot in upper left corner of N of ONE

RA   Horizontal scratch through upright and lower loop of P of PENNY

SA   Burr rub in value

SE   Blurred dot fairly close to left margin two-thirds way down

SL   Top line weak over GE

TD   Fresh entry value and POSTAGE

TG   Dot below S.W. corner of T and G squares

PLATE 15

Summary. Put to press 26.5.1855; defaced 1.5.1856; sheets printed not known, but estimated at 42,000; Alphabet II check letters; Imprimatur sheet in red-brown on paper almost free from blueing and watermarked small crown.

Colour. The majority of the printings were in red-brown on blued paper. Rarely a copper colour appears on deeply blued paper.

Perforation, 16 and 14; *Watermark,* Small and Large Crown. All combinations are known and the proportion works out at SC 16, 6%; SC 14, 25%; LC 16, 2%; LC 14, 67%.

Fresh entry. TJ is well marked.

Check letters. These are moderately well placed in their squares. The N.W. square is rather weak and noticeably so in late prints.

Note. The alignment of the plate is good.

AJ   Dot in upper left portion of O of POSTAGE

BG   Dot in S.W. corner of G square

BH   Short vertical scratch in top of H attached to cross bar

CC   Dot in centre of upright of P of POSTAGE

DH   Vertical scratch extends downwards to base line from upright of D

EC   Dot attached to base line beneath letter E

GA   Blurred dot in centre of Y

IE   Blurred dot in N.W. corner and dot in S.W. corner of I square

JJ   Burr rub N.W. square and PO

OD   Scratch and dot in margin below E of ONE

PB   Very large dot on temple

RD   Tiny dot below S.W. corner of R square

RJ   Very faint dot some distance below S.W. corner of J square

SD   Bottom line extends slightly on left

SG   Blurred mark in S.W. corner of s square

SL   Top line weak

TA   Lower right serif of T nearly absent

TG   Dot below S.W. corner of T square

TH   Dot below S.W. corner of T square

TJ   Fresh entry, POSTAGE and value

PLATE 16

Summary. Put to press 15.5.1855; defaced 22.6.1857; sheets printed not known, but estimated at 40,000; Alphabet II check letters; Imprimatur sheet in red-brown on paper slightly blued and watermarked small crown.

Colour. The majority of the printings are in a lighter shade of red-brown than the preceding plates. A milky brown colour is quite usual. The coppery colour on blued paper is scarce. The plate was still in use during the transitional period of early 1857. It can have been used but very little. The last printings were thus in a pale red colour on toned paper. They are very rare.

Perforation, 14; *Watermark,* Small and Large Crown. The combinations work out at SC 14, 6%; LC 14, 94%.

Fresh entries. NG, OE, TD. The latter is well marked.

Check letters. These are moderately well placed in their squares. The N.W. square is nearly always weak; POSTAGE and N.E. square show this tendency in late printings.

Notes. The alignment of the plate is irregular, showing a gradual rise from left to right on the printings. Wide and narrow spacings are frequent. There is an unusually wide space between LB and MB.

PLATE 16   59

A remarkable repair has been effected on AF and BF. As a result of burr rub ONE PENNY became spread out. Hand retouch to the base line has partly cut off the lower part of ONE.

AB	Dot below S.W. corner of B square	DD	Burr rub in N.W. square and POSTAGE

AF	Extremely marked burr rub ONE P; the base line has been strengthened by hand; the lower portion is partly cut off by this procedure; marks in N.W. square	DE	Big dot on top margin between N.W. square and P
		DF	Burr rub value
		DL	Large dot below S.W. corner of L square
AG	Tiny dot below S.W. corner of G square		
BC	Several tiny dots in margin above	EB	Dot below S.W. corner of B square
		EF	Burr rub value
		EH	Dot in S.W. corner of H square

BF	Marked burr rub value; the base line has been strengthened by hand causing the lower portion of ONE to be eliminated	EI	Dot below S.W. corner of I square; short vertical mark attached to base line near S.W. corner
		FK	Slight burr rub POSTAGE; tiny dot below S.W. corner of K square

		GG	First G recut and enlarged
CE	Dot after top right serif of E and dot on shoulder	HB	Several dots and short horizontal line in top of H square
CF	Marked burr rub value	HG	Dot below S.W. corner of G square
		HJ	Dot below S.W. corner of J square
CL	Tiny dot above A	IG	Dot below S.W. corner of G square

DB	Mark in S	II	Dot in front of first I

IK Dot below S.W. corner of K
    square

JH Mark on hair below crown

KB Dot below S.W. corner of K
    square

KJ Dot near N.W. corner of J
    square

LD Different punch for D used; D
    wider than normal

LJ J very faint

MB Different punch for B used; B
    larger than normal

MD Different punch for D used; D
    wider than normal

ME Short thin horizontal line in
    N.E. corner of M square

MG Vertical blur in S.W. corner of
    M square

MK Dot below S.W. corner of K
    square

ND Different punch for D used; D
    wider than normal

NE N and E faint

NG Coincident re-entry; G recut
    and enlarged; letter N faint
    from compression

OB Short vertical stroke in N.W.
    corner of O square; different
    punch for B used; B larger
    than normal

OD Horizontal scratch across tip
    of bust

OE Fresh entry marks in margin
    below

OG G recut and enlarged

PB Different punch for B used; B
    larger than normal

PH Loop of P enlarged; H slightly
    thinned

PJ Bottom line extends slightly
    on left

PK Large dot below S.W. corner of
    P square

QG G recut and enlarged

RD Tiny dot below S.W. corner of
    R square

SD Bottom line of D square weak

SG Blurred mark in S.W. corner of
    S square

SH Large dot below S.W. corner of
    S square

TA N.E. square weak

TB Top line weak over TAGE and
    N.E. square

TD Fresh entry all squares POS-
    TAGE and value; check let-
    ters thinned

TG Dot below S.W. corner of G
    square

TI Dot below S.E. corner of T
    square

TJ Dot below S.W. corner of T
    square

TL N.W. square weak

PLATE 17   61

PLATE 17

Summary. Put to press 15.5.1855; defaced 22.6.1857; sheets printed not known but estimated at 80,000; Alphabet II check letters; Imprimatur sheet in light red-brown on paper nearly free from blueing and water-marked small crown.

Colour. A few sheets were printed in a coppery colour on blued paper. The majority of the printings were in red-brown on blued paper. A milky brown is quite frequent. The plate was still in use during the transitional period of early 1857. It can have been used but very little. The last printings were thus in a pale red colour on toned paper. They are very rare.

Perforation, 14; *Watermark,* Small and Large Crown. The combination works out at SC 14, 3%; LC 14, 97%.

Check letters. These are reasonably well placed in their squares. Three separate punches were used in the T row. That for TB and TI is small; for TA, TC, TJ, TK and TL it is slightly larger; the punch used for TD, TE, TF, TG and TH is large and similar to Plate 6.

Notes. The alignment of the plate is reasonably good. There are no fresh entries.

CK	Short horizontal scratch in N.E. corner of c square very close to top	PA	Right side extends slightly above
	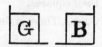	PJ	Large dot below S.W. corner of J square
GB	Dot within letter G and break in top of B	PK	Dot above upper right serif of K
		QG	Tiny dot below S.E. corner of G square
HL	Horizontal mark in back of G	QH	Tiny dot below S.E. corner of G square
IB	Dot in top of N of ONE		
IC	Bottom line extends slightly on right		
JA	Dot below and to right of top right serif of J		
KK	Dot in S.E. corner of first K square	QK	Large mark on ear
OE	Tiny dot below S.W. corner of o square	RK	R very high to right side of square which is irregular; left side extends slightly above

SI   Large dot in margin attached close to N.W. corner of N.E. square

SL   Top line weak over GE

TD   Dot below S.W. corner of D square

TE   Dot below S.W. corner of T square

TI   Large dot in margin below E of ONE

TK   Dot below S.W. corner of T square

PLATE 18

Summary. Put to press 1.6.1855; defaced 22.6.1857; sheets printed not known, but estimated at 20,000; Alphabet II check letters; Imprimatur sheet in light red-brown on paper nearly free from blueing and water-marked small crown.

Colour. The majority of the printings were in a deeper red-brown than usual on blued paper. The coppery colour on blued paper is more often seen. The plate was still in use during the transitional period of early 1857. It can have been used but very little. The last printings were thus in a pale red colour on toned paper. They are very rare.

Perforation, 14; *Watermark*, Small and Large Crown. The combinations work out at SC 14, 16%; LC 14, 84%.

Check letters. Reasonably accurately placed in their squares.

Notes. The alignment of the plate is reasonably good. There is the usual rise from left to right.

There are no fresh entries.

IB   Dot after centre of back of B

LJ   Large dot behind nostril

PI   Different punch used; P has a smaller loop than normal

PL   Different punch used; P has a smaller loop than normal

QG   Different punch for G used; G smaller than normal

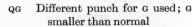

QL   L double below

RL   Dot below S.W. corner of L square

TE   Dot below S.W. corner of T square

TL   Dot below S.W. corner of T square

PLATE 19   63

PLATE 19

Summary. Put to press 16.10.1855; defaced 8.5.1856; sheets printed 26,000; Alphabet II check letters; Imprimatur sheet in red-brown on paper almost free from blueing and watermarked small crown.

Colour. The majority of the printings were in a deeper shade of red-brown on blued paper than is usual. The coppery colour on blued paper is more often seen.

Perforation, 14; *Watermark,* Small and Large Crown. The combination works out at SC 14, 19%; LC 14, 81%.

Check letters. Reasonably placed in their squares.

Notes. The alignment of the plate is irregular with wide and narrow margins frequent. GE is considerably misplaced upwards and very near FE. FH and FI are very nearly touching. There is the usual rise from left to right.

There are no fresh entries.

BH   Dot in centre of E of PENNY

DL   Large dot below and to right of D almost touching bottom line

ED   Tiny dot below S.W. corner of D square

JL   Two dots after top of J

LH   Small vertical scratch in margin just above H square

MJ   Dot in upper right serif of N of ONE

NJ   Large dot in S.W. corner of J square

OE   Large spot on front of shoulder

RG   Dot attached to left edge of serif of letter G

RK   Tiny dot outside corner of R square

SA   Dot below S.W. corner of S square

SJ   Large dot above s of POSTAGE

TE   Dot below S.W. corner of T square

TH   Dot close to S.W. corner of H square

TI   Dot below S.W. corner of T square

PLATE 20

Summary. Put to press 19.10.1855; defaced 8.5.1856; sheets printed 36,000; Alphabet II check letters; Imprimatur sheet in red-brown on paper slightly blued and watermarked small crown.

Colour. The majority of the printings were in a red-brown shade on blued paper. The coppery colour is not often seen but the milky brown colour is often encountered.

Perforation, 14; *Watermark,* Small and Large Crown. The combination works out at SC 14, 14%; LC 14, 86%.

Notes. The alignment of the plate is moderately good, but there is the usual slight rise from left to right.

There are no fresh entries.

AH   Dot in S.W. corner of H square

BL   Left side strengthened by hand retouch

CL   Left side strengthened by hand retouch

KG   Serif of G lengthened

KK   Tiny break at S.W. corner of second K square; tiny dot below S.W. corner of second K square

DJ   Large dot attached to bottom line of D square near S.E. corner

DL   Left side strengthened by hand retouch

LD   Dot below S.W. corner of L square

EL   Left side strengthened by hand retouch

OA   Side line of N.E. square weak

OG   Blur within G

FG   Dot in S.W. corner of G square

OI   Tiny dot in top of S

PI   Large dot below S.W. corner of P square

FL   Left side strengthened by hand retouch

QJ   Tiny dot in S.W. corner of J square

RH   Tiny dot in S.E. corner of H square

RI   Dot in S.E. corner of R square

HH   Two diagonal thick scratches on nose and two spots below eye

KD   Horizontal scratch below and to right of lower right serif of K

SI   Large spot on top of chest

TI   Bottom line extends on left

PLATE 21   65

PLATE 21

Summary. Put to press 8.6.1855; defaced 8.5.1856; sheets printed 29,000; Alphabet II check letters; Imprimatur sheet in red-brown on paper almost free from blueing and watermarked small crown.

Colour. The majority of the printings were in a deep red-brown shade on blued paper. The coppery colour is often seen on deeply blued paper.

Perforation, 14; *Watermark,* Small and Large Crown. The combination works out at SC 14, 14%; LC 14, 86%.

Check letters. Reasonably accurately placed in their squares.

Notes. The alignment of the plate is more accurate than usual.
There are no fresh entries.

AB	Dot in S.W. corner of B square	KE	Blurred dot after centre of K and tiny mark attached to lower right serif of K
AE	Dot in S.W. corner of E square		
BD	Large dot in S.W. corner of D square	QB	Dot in S.W. corner of B square
BF	Large dot in S.W. corner of F square		

RJ   Large dot above eye

GG   Mark very close to upper right serif of second G

IJ   Bottom line extends on left

TF   Letter F very tall and large as a result of hand retouch

E

TABLE OF RARITY

The following table shows the proportionate rarity of the One Penny Die II Alphabet II, grouped under the two watermarks and the two perforations. It is based on an examination of some 15,000 stamps. The quantities indicate the estimated proportion of each plate per 100,000 stamps.

Plate	SC 16	SC 14	LC 14	LC 16	Total
1	1568	1128	2712	200	5608
2	1608	1520	2392	168	5688
3	688	1280	224	8	2200
4	1912	1944	3600	184	7640
5	2192	1728	2880	192	6992
6	2128	1624	3208	112	7072
7	1264	1176	3696	160	6296
8	872	1192	3240	128	5432
9	1008	1448	3736	144	6336
10	768	784	2904	192	4648
11	528	912	3672	200	5312
12	792	1192	3696	168	5848
13	160	680	3280	96	4216
14	472	912	4352	160	5896
15	104	616	2648	56	3424
16	—	144	3224	16	3384
17	—	128	5656	—	5784
18	—	216	1176	—	1392
19	—	312	1616	—	1928
20	—	328	2728	—	3056
21	—	248	1600	—	1848
Total	16,604	19,512	62,240	2,184	100,000

Chapter Four

Fourth Issue of One Penny Perforated

DIE II: ALPHABET THREE

PLATES 22 to 68 and R17

Plate 22, the first with Alphabet III, and Plate 21, the last with Alphabet II, were registered on the 8th June, 1855 on the small crown paper, but Plate 22 was only put to press in August.

Plates 23, 25, 26, and R17 to R19 on the large crown paper, and Plates 24 and R20 on the small crown paper, were registered on the 12th November, 1855. But the large crown paper must have been put into use in the first months of 1855, as One Penny stamps on this paper exist with May dates. The small crown paper was therefore still in use after the first plates with Alphabet III were put to press, and the supply was not exhausted until some months later. Thus stamps with Alphabet III, which normally have the large crown watermark, may be found with the small crown. Used copies are scarce and unused examples exceedingly rare.

Stamps on the small crown paper from Plates 22 to 25 and 27 have been identified, and other stamps later than Plate 24 are known. They are all from the Gothic K plates.

Normally all plates with Alphabet III should be on the large crown paper.

Type I   Type II

Until 1861 the One Penny appeared with the Type I large crown watermark, and from 1861 with the Type II large crown.

Plates 22 to 68 and R17 had Alphabet III, and in 1861 Plates 50 and 51 appeared with Alphabet IV, while in 1862 Alphabet II again appeared on Plates R15 and R16.

The perforations at first were 14 and 16, and from 1856 the 14 perforation was used, but from the end of December 1857 to May 1858 the 16 gauge was again used to a limited extent.

WATERMARK LARGE CROWN: TYPE I

The following grouping arises out of the many, but unintentional, shades of the red colour which have been met with in the two preceding issues on the small crown paper, and which appear again in the early printings on the large crown paper.

During the latter half of 1856 there was a definite attempt to change the composition of the ink in order to eliminate the blueing of the paper. The use of prussiate of potash was abandoned, and towards the end of 1856 stamps appeared on paper free from blueing, which finally ceased from March 1857.

These red-brown shades on paper free from blueing are very rare indeed and, unfortunately, are easily faked. Specimens should be on a dated piece bearing November and December 1856 dates. Plates 27, 32, 35 and 44 have been identified in this rare red-brown colour.

The stamps of Type I on the large crown paper may, therefore, be divided into three groups:

    (a) In the old red-brown shades on blued paper.

    (b) Intermediate, or transition period.

    (c) In rose-red on paper free from blueing.

In the transitional period (b) there were intermediate printings, more or less experimental, on a yellowish-toned paper, in which the old red-brown shade appeared, and also the early rose shades from which the rose-red issue developed. The continual colour changes during the first part of 1857 and the yellowish-toned paper were probably due to attempts to produce fugitive inks without the addition of prussiate of potash, and possibly to the use of a neutralizing agent in the paper.

The early printings of group (c) from April 1857 appear in pale rose shades, and the normal rose-red appeared in July. This ended in a rich carmine-rose before the end of the year, and was maintained throughout the issue except for short periods about 1862, when pale shades varying little from the pale rose of April–July, 1857 again appeared at intervals.

By dividing this issue into these three groups it is possible to treat the rose-red shades as a separate group.

This grouping does not correspond to a plate grouping, as Alphabet III plates of Group (a) were used in the other two groups, and the plate grouping is therefore subordinate to this other form of division, which is even more important, and shows more obvious differences.

The imprimatur sheets from 1856 to the beginning of 1858 show that Plates 43 to 51, registered on the 25th June, 1856, were for the last time in the red-brown colour of Group (a), on blued paper. Plates 52, 53, 55 to 60, registered on the 11th February, 1857, were in the orange-red colour of Group (*b*), on unblued paper, and Plates 61 to 68, registered on the 15th January, 1858, were in the rich carmine-rose of Group (*c*).

Group (*a*); red-brown shades on blued paper

PLATES 1 to 21

These are fully dealt with on pp. 28 to 66.

PLATES 22 to 48

This sub-group comprises all the One Penny plates from 22 onwards with Alphabet III, which still appeared in the old colours of the small crown blued paper. Plate 47, however, is the last one of which a considerable number of examples have been seen on decidedly blued paper. It was put to press on the 15th December, 1856, which agrees with the assumption that the experiments with colours without the addition of potassium prussiate, and with chemical treatment of the paper, began towards the end of 1856. Stamps from Plate 48, which was put to press on the 2nd February, 1857, were undoubtedly printed in the pale red shade, but the blueing was not strong. On the other hand the imprimatur sheets of Plates 52, 53 and 55 to 60, registered on the 11th February, 1857, were printed in the new orange-red colour of the transition period on uncoloured paper, and it therefore appears probable that during the transition period, in addition to the experiments with new colours, the use of the old inks without chemical treatment of the paper was continued for a time.

As plates from 22 onwards were first put to press in November 1855 the stamps of this sub-group no longer appeared normally with perforation 16, and apart from other perforation varieties, imperforate stamps were from time to time inadvertently issued, examples of which are known, including a pair on the original cover. Unused examples have not yet been found.

Plates 27, 34, 36 to 39 and 41 to 48 were also used for the rose-red issue. Of these there is considerable material available, including unused blocks, etc, and they will be considered under Group (*c*), which comprises the later rose-red issue Plates 49 to 68.

Plates 22, 23 and 24 were laid down simultaneously in June 1855, and consequently have certain characteristics in common. Plates 23 and 24, however, were apportioned to the reserve plates, and were re-numbered R17 and R18. R17 was used in 1862 for the rose-red printing. New plates were laid down in November 1855, along with Plates 25 and 26, and were again numbered 23 and 24. Consequently Plates 22 and R17 (originally Plate 23) have the characteristic letters E, H, K, L, M, S, described and illustrated under Group (c), the most remarkable of which is the semi-Gothic K which forms the transition to the Gothic K of the later plates. It differs from the latter by the oblique lines being joined to the vertical one by a short horizontal bar. The Gothic K is the characteristic letter of following plates.

The S is large on Plates 22 and 23.

The large L on Plate 23, and the horizontal row of Plate 24, bears a similarity to that found on Plates 22 and R17. Plate 25 has the small L, which appears up to Plate 55.

RE-ENTRIES

The following re-entries are illustrated:

AA	Plate 30	HD	Plate 40	LE	Plate 28
AC	Plate 30	GL/HL	Plate 28	MF	Plate 28
CE	Plate 22	IE	Plate 25	NL	Plate 28
EK/FK	Plate 24	KC/LC	Plate 23	PK/QK	Plate 29
FG	Plate 31	KI	Plate 28	RL/SL	Plate 32

FL has prominent markings which are evidently due to considerable damage to the plate. It may be found in many shades, but only on the blue paper.

Group (b); transition colours on yellowish paper

The stamps of this group, unlike those of the previous groups on blued or grey-white paper, were printed on yellowish or creamy toned paper.

The experiments to prevent blueing appear to have been two-fold. Firstly attempts were made to provide fugitive inks with prussiate of potash added, the reaction of which gave the blueing; secondly to neutralize this reaction by the use of other agents such as 'antichlor', which probably accounted for the yellow tint. The experiment began before the end of 1856, and continued during the first months of 1857, and the printings therefrom were put into circulation in or before March 1857.

The first experimental issues in red-brown, orange-brown and orange-red were small, and these shades are accordingly scarce; the later issues in light red and pale rose were more plentiful. From April 1857, there appeared along with the pale rose stamps on yellowish paper, similar shades on the uncoloured paper of Group (c). Towards July 1857 the early rose shades lost the washy appearance, and the paper was uniformly uncoloured.

Group (c); the rose-red issue

Plates between 27 and 53, 55 to 68 and reserve Plate 17.

The stamps of this issue are common, but in the past their study was neglected, except as regards those with Alphabets II and IV, which were sought for by earlier collectors, as they were easily recognized, and there were only four plates.

The stamps with Alphabet III have come into prominence owing mainly to the pioneer work of Dr Gordon Ward, who established the grouping of the plates, which has simplified the identification of the stamps, and the reconstruction of plates. Some of his notes were published in the *British Philatelist* of 1923.

The alphabets of this group may be divided into three sub-groups:

(1) 1857–64. Plates 27, 31, 33 to 39, 41 to 49, 52, 53, 55 to 68 and R17 with Alphabet III.

(2) 1861–64. Plates 50, 51, with Alphabet IV.

(3) 1862–64. Plates R15, R16, with Alphabet II.

From 1857 to 1861 only plates with Alphabet III were used, the majority of which had already been used for Group (a).

From 1861/62 onwards the Alphabet III plates were supplemented by the plates of the sub-groups 2 and 3, while the plates for the One Penny new Type III were being laid down.

The printing in rose-red on white paper, which first appeared in April 1857, was the first practical result of the experimental printings made to eliminate the discolouring of the paper.

The early printings were in pale rose shades, and in July a rich rose-red appeared, which developed into a deep carmine-rose. There were, however, variations from the normal carmine, and even brownish tones exist which have been confused with earlier issues.

Later printings again appeared in rose pink, particularly in 1862, and stamps from Plates 50, 51, R15, R16, and R17 may be found in a weak insipid colour.

These plates produced large quantities of sheets; for instance, Plate 27 printed over one million. In February 1872, after it had been superseded by a new type, Perkins, Bacon were permitted to make a print of it in black on thin card for exhibition purposes. They retained this for over sixty years, and when the firm was dissolved in January 1936 the sheet was sold and has now been broken up.

The carmine shades are readily acted on by sulphur compounds, and are therefore frequently discoloured. The familiar remedy is a solution of hydrogen peroxide, which oxidizes the black sulphide into colourless sulphate.

Perforation 14 was used, as the 16 gauge was discontinued about the end of 1855, but before the end of 1857 a reserve perforation 16 comb was put into use for a short period, and consequently stamps from plates at press about this time may be found with both perforations.

The following plates have been identified: 27, 34, 36, 37, 38, 42 to 49, 52, 55 to 60.

As the rose-red stamps with perforation 16 are known dated the 29th December, 1857, and the 2nd January, 1858, the provisional use of the 16 comb appears to have lasted over four months, as dated specimens mostly cease after May 1858. Stamps with this perforation are usually badly centred, and therefore perfect examples are scarce.

Evidently a few imperforate sheets were put into circulation in error, and examples are known from Plates 41, 42, 52, 55, 57, 60, 62, 66, R17 and 51. These cannot be from the imprimatur sheets, as some are unused with gum, and most are in different shades from the imprimatur printings. Pairs and strips of three are known.

Examples may be found with double and even triple perforations.

The Type I large crown watermark was used until 1861, when it was generally replaced by Type II. Plates 66 and 67, which came into use in 1861, are commonly found with both types, but earlier plates, still at press in 1861 (52–64), sometimes have the second type, while the latter plates, including Plates 50 and 51, are occasionally found with the first type. The paper in stock at this time was evidently served out indiscriminately.

From 1863 mould letters* were added to the marginal watermark, and the crown errors on MA and TA appear on various plates from 48 onwards, and also on Plate R16.

It has been stated that in 1864 a request was made to the postal authorities, on behalf of junior members of the Royal Family, for examples of the One Penny black of 1840. As none of these were available a printing in black was made from a plate then at press. Plate 66, Die II with Alphabet III, was used for this purpose, and the stamps were printed on the large crown paper, imperforate, and with the watermark inverted.

Some blocks and strips exist, and examples which come on the market are in great demand.

At the same time a printing was made in carmine, also imperforate, but with the watermark normal.

Plates 27, 31, 33 to 38 and 42 to 49 were still in use at the end of the transition period, and of these 31 and 35 appeared only in the earliest shades, as they were defaced in June 1857. Plates 33, 37, 38 and 45 outlived the initial stages of this issue, and very few examples are known, although they were not destroyed until October 1861. Plate 40, also defaced in June 1857, was evidently out of use at this period.

* See *Great Britain 1840-53*, now known as *Part One* (Second Edition), p. 68.

Thirty-five different plates with Alphabet III were used, which will be described later.

The printing in this issue as a rule does not show the clean-cut hardness of the early printings with Alphabet I, and the paper appears to be of a softer texture, causing the ink to spread. The check letters are fairly uniform, with a few marked exceptions, which are described.

Double letters are few and are usually inconspicuous; in some cases the letters have been re-cut, especially the G's. A large number of impressions show constant accidental marks of small importance, except for plating. These marks in a block or strip may identify the plate, and form a key-piece by which the plating may be carried on by overlapping with other blocks or strips, and therefore these minor varieties are illustrated.

Many mint blocks fortunately exist, in some cases with margins showing plate numbers.

ALPHABET III

This set of letters is a complex one, but it is conveniently grouped under the general heading of Alphabet III. The letters are generally taller and more slender than those of Alphabet II, but there are some marked differences between similar letters.

The following illustrations show the general appearance of the letters which have marked changes:

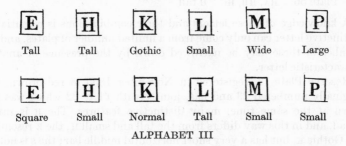

| E | H | K | L | M | P |
| Tall | Tall | Gothic | Small | Wide | Large |

| E | H | K | L | M | P |
| Square | Small | Normal | Tall | Small | Small |

ALPHABET III

A number of different punches was employed for each letter, many having slight differences. This can be discerned on several plates in which a letter alters in appearance from one impression to the next.

The different appearance is also due to the position in which the punch was held before being struck with the hammer. If not quite vertical a slightly unequal impression would be made on the plate, producing for example weak serifs on one side of the letter and strong serifs on the other.

Alphabet III can be conveniently sub-divided into the following headings:

(a) Tall B, Tall E, Tall H, Gothic K, Short L, Broad M, P large loop.
(b) Tall B, Tall E, Tall H, Short L, Broad M, P large loop.
(c) Tall B, Tall E, Tall H, Short L, Narrow M, P large loop.
(d) Tall B, Tall E, Tall H, Short L, Narrow M, P small loop.
(e) Broad B, Broad E, Tall H, Short L, Narrow M, P small loop.
(f) Broad B, Broad E, Tall H, Tall L, Narrow M, P small loop.
(g) Broad B, Broad E, Small H, Tall L, Narrow M, P small loop.

Plates 22 and R17 have the following characteristic letters:

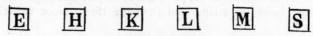

Characteristic Letters of Reserve Plate 17

ALPHABET III

Under each plate separately described is stated the sub-group of Alphabet III to which it belongs. There are a few exceptions which can be mentioned here; they are also separately described under the plate heading.

Plate 23.   LL   First L tall, second L short
Plate 31.   RK   Gothic K retouched by hand to appear normal
Plate 37.   MJ, MK, ML   M narrow
Plate 46.   PJ, PK, PL   P has small loop
Plate 56.   HA, HB, HC   H tall.

A knowledge of these letters and their combinations is essential. A distinctive letter can only come from a limited number of plates, and the number of these may be narrowed down by the presence of another characteristic letter.

Reserve Plate 17, registered in November 1855 in red-brown, was originally numbered 23 and has, jointly with Plate 22 which was laid down at the same time, many distinctive features. The H is rather broad, and in this way differs from the tall and small H; the K resembles the Gothic K, but has a very short horizontal middle bar; the s is noticeably larger than the normal s of Alphabet III, and has an open top loop.

The plates covered by this group up to Plate 47 were put to press before the end of 1856, and at least the first issues were made in red-brown on blued paper. Plates 48 and 49, put to press on the 2nd February, 1857 and the 3rd April, 1857 respectively, are rarely seen in red-brown but never any later plates. Plate 52 was put to press on the 7th May, 1857; Plate 53 on the 12th February, 1857; Plate 55 on the 21st May, 1857; Plates 56 to 60 on the 7th July, 1857; Plate 61 on the 5th May, 1858; Plate 62 on the 12th December, 1859; Plate 63 on the 3rd

March, 1860; Plate 64 on the 5th November, 1860; Plate 65 on the 14th January, 1861; Plates 66 and 67* on the 13th February, 1861; and Plate 68 on the 9th January, 1862.

These dates are given by Wright and Creeke and are important as it is obvious that stamps which show early dates must necessarily belong to a limited range of plates.

RE-ENTRIES

Many good examples of re-entries may be found among the rose-red plates with Alphabet III, and most of those which are reasonably prominent are illustrated.

Others less prominent, some of which may probably not be re-entries, are included with the minor varieties to be referred to later.

Most of these varieties up to Plate 47 exist also in the red-brown shades of the 1856 printing.

One of the most popular, and also the commonest, is the AD-BD re-entry of Plate 27, which may be found in the following states:

1. (Abnormal) Red-brown on blued paper; Small crown watermark
2. (Abnormal) Red-brown on blued paper; Large crown watermark
3. Light red, and on the other transitional shades
4. Rose-red; Large crown, perforation 14
5. Rose-red; Large crown, perforation 16

Plate 55 provides a large number of re-entries, and evidently the whole of the A, B and C vertical rows were re-entered, as most of these stamps show some indication of the double impression. Many are very feeble, but usually there is some trace to be seen in the N.E. corner, which generally shows a horizontal line in the lower arm of the cross. A mark in the O of ONE is also a common feature.

Plate 62 has a prominent group in the lower right-hand corner of the sheet. But possibly the strongest and the scarcest re-entries are those from Plate 64. The very rare fresh entries are from Plate 65.

		Plate 55.	AA, AB, AC, AD, BA, BB, BC,
Plate 27.	AD, BD		CA, CB, CC, DA, DB, DC,
Plate 37.	BI		EA, EB, EC, FA, FB, FC,
Plate 42.	AA		GA, GB, GC, HA, HB, HC,
Plate 43.	RJ		HD, IA, IB, IC, JA, JB, JC,
Plate 46.	BH, LI		KA, KB, KC, LA, LB, LC,
Plate 48.	BG		MA, MB, MC, NA, NB,
Plate 49.	AD		NC, OA, OB, OC, PA, PB,
			PC, QA, QB, QC, RA, RB,
			RC, RD, SA, SB, SC, TA,
			TB, TC, TD

* Wright and Creeke give the year for Plate 67 as 1862. This is evidently a misprint, as copies used in 1861 are known.

Plate 56.   DG, GJ
Plate 57.   BJ
Plate 59.   CI, QG, RG, TF
Plate 60.   BI, FB, OC
Plate 61.   SL

Plate 62.   LK, PJ, QJ, RC, RJ, SF, SJ, SL, TJ, TK, TL
Plate 64.   TB, TC, TD, TL
Plate 65.   RL, TL
Plate 68.   AG, IE, IF, JE, JF, KL, NC
Plate R17. JF, RI

DOUBLE-LETTERS

Very few clearly defined double letters are to be found in this issue. Various impressions show marks resembling them, but these are questionable, and therefore they are included with the constant marks. Possibly the most satisfactory examples are:

AH	Plate	47	EH	Plate	57	OC	Plate	39
CD	,,	58	FC	,,	60	OE	,,	R17
DJ	,,	R17	GD	,,	48	RJ	,,	44
EC	,,	47	GE	,,	46	SC	,,	59
EF	,,	39	ML	,,	57			

EXTENDED FRAME LINES

Minute extensions often seem to exist, but are frequently delusive, and are usually due to the texture of the paper which caused the ink to spread. Definite examples are not very numerous, and proved ones form valuable plating clues, but perforation holes and bad centring are disadvantages.

RETOUCHES and CONSTANT MARKS

Many of these are trifling, but when definitely established form valuable plating clues, and are mainly given as such.

They may be classified as follows:

1. Re-entry marks due to a second application of the roller, and the incomplete erasure of the faulty impression.
2. Incised marks such as retouches, defective re-cutting, slipping of the graving tool, and accidental cuts and scratches. Some of these appear only in later states of the plates, but are given when they may be commonly found.
3. Marks due to burrs, corrosion, or wear and tear. As these vary considerably according to the state of the plates, they are consequently not permanent features, and are therefore generally excluded. Curved burrs are frequently found against the circular letters C, G and O.
4. Accidental spots and blots caused by smudges and splashes of ink

during the printing. These are not plate varieties, and do not recur on stamps with the same lettering. They are numerous and usually occur at the edge of the plate.

PLATE 22

Summary. Put to press 1.8.1855; defaced 22.6.1857; sheets printed 7,000; Imprimatur sheet in a plum shade on blued paper watermarked small crown.

Colour. The printings are usually red-brown on blued paper. The earliest specimens were in a copper colour on deeply blued paper watermarked small crown.

Watermark and Perforation. Both Large and Small Crown, the former just predominates. Perforation 14.

Check letters. The plate is full of interest, as it contains some characteristic letters. The s is unusually tall and similar to that on Plate 23; the E is small, thin and has a 'broken back' appearance with pronounced serifs, and the middle bar is placed too high; the L is tall, thin and has a 'broken back' appearance, the lower bar falling downwards to form an obtuse angle. The letter K is semi-Gothic, the lower horizontal bar being placed slightly high so as to join the upper bar distal to the upright; H is squat, rather broad, and somewhat larger than the H of sub-group (*g*).

Notes. As the printing was so small examples are very scarce and a total reconstruction is probably impossible. Centring is often unkind and must have led to many stamps being discarded.

This plate was used by Perkins, Bacon for a trial printing on a steam-driven press.* A complete sheet so printed was in existence up to 1960, having come to light in America, but has since been cut up. It had an inscription in ink on the four margins, twice in English and twice in French, which reads: 'This sheet is one of 2000 printed by Mr Neale's machine for us this day August 15, 1855.' The trial was not considered successful and printing by hand was resumed. Very few dated copies have been seen; these extend between March and July 1856.

GE	Both letters retouched by hand; the E has lost its characteristic appearance and the G has been enlarged with a long horizontal serif	
CE	Fresh entry upper squares, POSTAGE and value	
FI	Mark in front of I	
HI	H double	
RB	Bottom line extends so as to touch R square of RC	

* *Line-Engraved Postage Stamps of Great Britain*, p. 144.

Note: The following illustrations
show the characteristic letters in the
s row

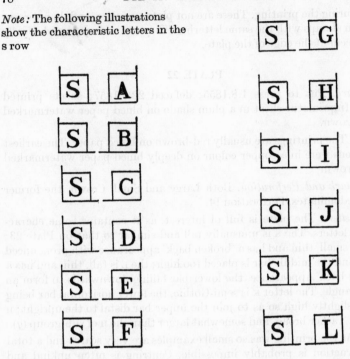

PLATE 23

Summary. Put to press 17.11.1855; defaced 22.6.1857; sheets printed 62,000; Imprimatur sheet in a plum shade on blued paper watermarked large crown.

Colour. Usually creamy red-brown on blued paper. Early copies are in a copper colour on deeply blued paper.

Watermark and Perforation. Both Large and Small Crown, but copies with Small Crown are scarce and only represent a fraction of the total printings. Perforation 14.

Check Letters. The s is characteristic, being unusually tall and similar to that found on Plate 22; L is tall but differs from Plate 22 in that the lower bar is at right angles to the upper arm. The K is Gothic; the other letters conform to Alphabet III (*a*).

Notes. The printing is clear and a cameo-like head makes its appearance. The top line and POSTAGE is often slightly weak, and POSTAGE expanded through burr-rub.

This plate is exceedingly rare in mint condition, only one well-centred small piece of eleven (now broken up) being known. The remainder are badly off-centre.

PLATE 23   79

AL	Dot to left of lower left serif of L in early printings only; tall L very high central	NK	Dot below left leg of N
CC	Large dot in margin over AGE		
CF	Top line weak	OD	o double
DL	Top line weak		
EL	Short horizontal stroke below L visible in early printings only		
KF	Strong blur connects S.E. corner of F square to N.E. corner of N.E. square of LF	PE	Blurred mark in front of neck
		QH	Top line very weak over TAGE
MH	Burr rub POSTAGE	TD	Top line weak

PLATE 24

Summary. Put to press 24.11.1855; defaced 22.6.1857; sheets printed 80,000; Imprimatur sheet in red-brown on slightly blued paper watermarked small crown.

Colour. Red-brown on blued paper: the cameo-like head appears but is scarce. Copies in a copper colour on deeply blued paper, watermarked small crown, are scarce.

Watermark and Perforation. Large Crown and Small Crown, perforated 14. Small Crown printings are scarce and represent a fraction of the total printed.

Check Letters. L is both tall and short on this plate. In the horizontal row LA to LI inclusive and LK, the L is tall; LJ has a short L; LL has the first L tall and the second short; the vertical L row has all L's short. This LL is the only one in the entire series to show differing types of the same letter.

The K is Gothic: the lettering conforms to Alphabet III (a).

Note. Mint pieces are unknown with the Small Crown watermark and single copies are very rare.

		KJ	Scratch runs through outer side of N.E. square
EK	Fresh entry marks letter squares and value		
FK	Fresh entry marks letter squares and POSTAGE	LJ	Dot to left of top left serif of L (short L)

LL   First L tall, second L short   OP   Similar to OH

MG   Spot on face   PI   Misplaced letters

OH   Mark below and to left of O,
      probably trace of double
      letter

PLATE 25

Summary. Put to press 12.11.1855; defaced 22.6.1857; sheets printed 45,000; Imprimatur sheet in reddish-brown on slightly blued paper watermarked large crown.

Colour. Red-brown on blued paper: cameo-heads are scarce. The printing was small and specimens are consequently rather scarce. A copper colour on deeply blued paper watermarked small crown is scarce. There was a very small printing at the end of the plate's life in transitional shades of red-brown on paper free from blueing.

Watermark and Perforation. Large Crown and Small Crown, perforation 14. Small Crown copies are scarce and only consist of a fraction of the total printing.

Check Letters. The K is Gothic; the lettering conforms to Alphabet III (*a*).

Notes. A half sheet (AA–JL), cut up long ago, exists imperforate. Mint pieces are unknown. There is a good re-entry on FK.

FK   Nearly coincident re-entry;   KF   Heavy blur upper half of right
      both letters weak, value   side
      slightly compressed

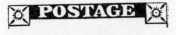

KL   L double

IE   Fresh entry all squares and
      value

KD   D faint

LG   L very high to right

PLATE 25   81

SJ   Dot in top of s

TD   Fresh entry upper squares,
      POSTAGE, value and below

PLATE 26

Summary. Put to press 12.11.1855; defaced 22.6.1857; sheets printed 40,000; Imprimatur sheet in reddish-brown on blued paper watermarked large crown.

Colour. Often a softer red-brown on blued paper. The creamy red-brown seen on Plate 23 appears frequently. The finest examples of the cameo-head appear from this plate.

Watermark and Perforation. Large Crown, perforation 14.

Check Letters. The K is Gothic; the lettering conforms to Alphabet III (*a*).

Notes. The printing is often clear and of splendid appearance. Specimens are however scarce as the printing was small. No mint pieces are known.

BA   Margin weak over AGE   RL   Top line weak

KH   Top line weak

MH   Burr rub POSTAGE; blurred
      mark after M   SE   s double

PLATE 27

Summary. Put to press 27.12.55; defaced—date unknown; sheets printed 1,011,900 of which about 140,000 were on blued paper; Imprimatur sheet in red-brown on blued paper watermarked large crown.

The plate was withdrawn from use on 22.3.61, but copies are frequent with 1862 and 1863 dates and may also be seen bearing dates of 1864, when the 'Star plates' were all withdrawn and replaced by the plate number series.

Colour and Watermark. The very early printings were in a bronze colour on markedly blued paper watermarked small crown. These are exceedingly rare. This is the last plate which may be found with small crown watermark. The printings are normally all on paper with large crown watermark. The depth of the brown colour varied but remains fairly constant as a red-brown on blued paper. Orange-brown shades on blued paper are scarce. In January 1857, the transitional colours appeared on yellowish to cream paper in a pale rose and pale red colour. Very few printings have been seen in red-brown on creamy paper. In April of the same year transitional shades appeared on white paper, and in the

F

following July the rose-red shade, which persisted to the end of life of these series of plates, appeared.

Perforation. This was normally 14. The 16 gauge was temporarily used in late December 1857 and from January to March 1858. Printings from this plate however with this perforation are uncommon.

Check Letters. These are Alphabet III (*a*), with κ Gothic.

Notes. The alignment of the plate is very accurate and well centred blocks exist. This plate contains the well-known 'Star AD–BD' re-entry, and is much sought after in red-brown on blue paper and in transitional and rose-red shades. Only two copies of AD have been reported perforated 16, and only one is known on the Small Crown paper.

In 1872, the plate still being in existence, Perkins Bacon were permitted to print a sheet in black for the Exhibition to be held at South Kensington. No plate number or marginal inscriptions were shown. The printing was made on a soft card.* This sheet was cut up twenty years ago.

The plate has a strong N.E. square throughout and the right side is strong and often blurred.

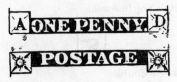

AD   Fine fresh entry letter squares and value

AH   Right side of H square curves outwards due to inaccurate punching of H

AL   Blur through upper part of E of POSTAGE

BD   Strong evidence of original entry of AD in upper squares and POSTAGE

BI   Small blurred mark in lower portion of O of POSTAGE

BL   Several small marks on shoulder

DI   Oblique blurred line through OS extends into margin above

EK   E hand cut and enlarged spot on tip of nose in early prints

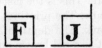

FJ   Coincident fresh entry; both letters hand cut and enlarged

* *Line-Engraved Postage Stamps of Great Britain*, p. 178.

PLATE 27   83

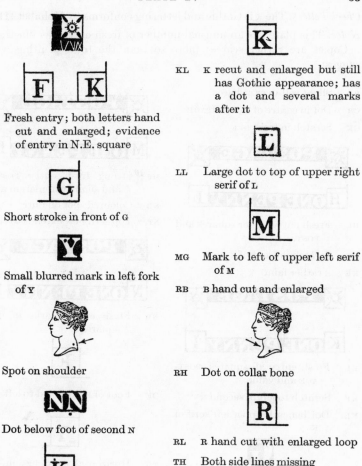

FK   Fresh entry; both letters hand cut and enlarged; evidence of entry in N.E. square

HG   Short stroke in front of G

JA   Small blurred mark in left fork of Y

JB   Spot on shoulder

JC   Dot below foot of second N

KF   Dot above upright of K

KJ   Upper half of left side missing

KL   K recut and enlarged but still has Gothic appearance; has a dot and several marks after it

LL   Large dot to top of upper right serif of L

MG   Mark to left of upper left serif of M

RB   B hand cut and enlarged

RH   Dot on collar bone

RL   R hand cut with enlarged loop

TH   Both side lines missing

TK   Gothic K very low central

PLATE 28

Summary. Put to press 27.12.1855; defaced 22.6.1857; sheets printed 76,000; Imprimatur sheet in reddish-brown on blued paper water-marked large crown.

Colour. This is fairly constant, being a clear red-brown on blued paper.

Watermark and Perforation. Always Large Crown, perforation 14.

Check Letters. The κ is Gothic and lettering conforms to Alphabet III (*a*).

Notes. This plate has an unusual number of fresh entries as illustrated.

Copies are rather scarce; more so than the total printing would suggest.

BA	Slight roll-over at base
CB	Dot in centre of s of POSTAGE
GK	Scratch in front of κ

HL	Fresh entry upper squares and POSTAGE
JK	Scratch in front of κ
KE	E rather faint

KI	Fresh entry all squares, POSTAGE and value
KK	Scratch to left of second κ
KL	Dot beneath upper left serif of κ

MF	Strong fresh entry POSTAGE and slightly in margin above
NB	Coloured spot on burr
NF	Top serif of N extends to right

NL	Fresh entry marks in upper squares

OF	Foot of F extended to left

TH	Horizontal scratches in S.W. corner of T square

LE	Dot in back of G of POSTAGE; fresh entry N.E. square
TJ	Short horiztonal line below T square

PLATE 29

Summary. Put to press 27.12.1855; defaced 22.6.1857; sheets printed 93,000; Imprimatur sheet in reddish-brown on blued paper water-marked large crown.

PLATE 29   85

Colour. Usually deep chocolate-brown on paper fairly heavily blued, but copies are also found in the normal red-brown on blued paper. Specimens showing an orange-brown tint are uncommon.

Watermark and Perforation. Always Large Crown, perforated 14.

Check Letters. The K is Gothic and the lettering conforms to Alphabet III (a).

BA   B with large loops

BJ   B double

KI   Top line extends on left

LG   Small mark to right and slightly below upper right serif of L; large spot on lower serif of L

LK   Top line extends on left

ME   Dot nearly attached to toe of E

ML   Tiny dot outside S.E. corner of M square; L low and far to right

NI   Fresh entry upper and lower squares and value

NJ   N very close to left side of square, and low

OI   Fresh entry, mostly in N.W. square

PI   Top line of I square irregular

PK   Several marks in K square; left side extends below

QK   Fresh entry upper squares and POSTAGE

RE   E double at top; nearly touching top margin of square

RH   Serifs of H joined top and bottom

SE   Coloured dot attached to base of E square below upright of E

SL   Burr rub POSTAGE

TB   Vertical stroke connects bottom right serif of T to base line

TG   Short vertical scratch in N.W. corner of T square

PLATE 30

Summary. Put to press 27.12.1855; defaced 22.6.1857; sheets printed 88,000; Imprimatur sheet in reddish-brown on blued paper watermarked large crown.

Colour. Almost invariably deep chocolate-brown on deeply blued paper, but copies can be seen in red-brown on blued paper.

Watermark and Perforation. Always Large Crown, perforated 14.

Check Letters. The K is Gothic and the lettering conforms to Alphabet III (*a*).

Note. Copies are rather scarce and often off-centre.

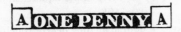

AA   Fresh entry upper squares

AC   Fresh entry upper squares and value

AK   Dot after top left serif of K

BC   Top line N.E. square weak and thin over E of POSTAGE

CE   E double

KB   Lower loop of B lengthened

MG   Top right serif of M extends to right

MJ   Vertical stroke in N.W. corner of J square attached to top margin

NF   F double above

OA   Dot in right side of O; lower curve of S in POSTAGE partly blotted out

PI   Blob of colour on left margin opposite neck

QB   B close to left side of square

PLATE 30   87

RD   Curved mark in front of D
RL   Dot and smudge within R

SG   Vertical stroke in N.W. corner
       of s square

TB   Dot in S.E. corner of B square;
       blurred dot outside T square
       below upright of T

TJ   Dot in loop of P of POSTAGE

PLATE 31

Summary. Put to press 27.12.1855; defaced 22.6.1857; sheets printed 160,000; Imprimatur sheet in reddish-brown on blued paper watermarked large crown.

Colour. Except for the long-lived Plate 27 this is the earliest plate in which transitional shades on toned paper freed from blueing may be found. The earliest printings are in a deep chocolate shade on deeply blued paper, followed by red-brown and orange-brown shades on paper not so deeply blued. Later the blueing became less marked.

Early in 1857 printings in pale red appeared on toned paper almost entirely free from blueing. These were followed by a pale red on toned paper which was entirely free. Finally the pale rose shade on toned paper appeared in May–June 1857, shortly before the plate was withdrawn, so that printings in rose-red do not exist. A few copies in orange on deeply blued paper may be seen.

Check Letters. The letters are sometimes difficult to identify and plating is not easy. While the K is Gothic, and the letters conform generally to Alphabet III (*a*) there is an interesting exception to the Gothic K's on this plate. RK has to all appearances a normal K, but close inspection reveals it as originally Gothic but retouched by hand to lose its characteristic appearance.

The late J. B. Seymour, when asked by Mr H. F. Johnson if he had a copy of RK Plate 31, replied that it was the only Gothic in the plate he had not identified. He was then shown a small mint block in pale rose on toned paper with sheet margins and Plate 31 in the corner, which cleared up the mystery. A used vertical strip containing RK has also been identified by Mr Johnson and up-to-date is unique.

Fresh Entries. There are two good fresh entries (EG–FG) and GI in which the G has also been retouched by hand and considerably enlarged.

Note. This is a rewarding plate to mount and show. The varieties of colours and depths of blueing together with the toned paper make a most attractive display.

DK   Marks in N.W. square

EG   Letters enlarged by hand retouch

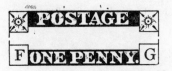

FG   Fresh entry upper squares and value; G recut and enlarged

GF   F double

GI   Fresh entry all squares, POSTAGE and value; G recut and enlarged

HK   Dot below upper left serif of K

LH   Marks on top of NE PE in late printings

MA   Spot on edge of neck

ND   Short vertical line in N.W. corner of D square

NK   Fresh entry N.W. square; large scratch in front of K

OF   Large dot to left of top left serif of F

OG   Mark at angle of jaw, becoming less marked on late printings; lower portion of curve of G defective

RB   Vertical scratch in N.W. corner of B square

RK   K retouched by hand to lose its Gothic appearance

TJ   Blurred mark to left of T in very late printings

TK   Spot on throat in later printings

PLATE 32

Summary. Put to press 8.2.1856; defaced 22.6.1857; sheets printed 130,000; Imprimatur sheet in reddish-brown on blued paper watermarked large crown.

PLATE 32   89

Colour. Usually chocolate-brown on fairly deeply blued paper in the early printings, becoming a normal red-brown on slightly blued paper later. The plate was used for the early transitional shade of pale red on toned paper, but shades of pale rose have not been seen. These are extremely scarce.

Watermark and Perforation. Always Large Crown, perforated 14.

Check Letters. Conform to Alphabet III (*b*).

Note. The plate wore badly, and late printings show much wear of the lateral borders and engine-turned background. Evidently no attempt at repair was made.

AK   Large dot in S.W. corner of K square

AL   Mark in top of hair

BC   Mark in mouth of C

BD   Large spot on nose

BG   Fresh entry upper squares, POSTAGE and margin below

BL   Scratch through lower corner of L square

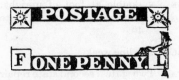

FL   Marks around L square

KA   Dot in centre of left fork of Y of PENNY

KH   Dot after top right serif of H, nearly touches right side

LF   Horizontal scratches in top of N.W. square

MJ   Blurred dot in S.E. corner of J square

MK   Dot in N.W. corner of K square

SL   Fresh entry upper squares and margin above

TI   Tiny dots below lower right serif of T

PLATE 33

Summary. Put to press probably in February 1856; defaced 29.10.1861; sheets printed 138,000; Imprimatur sheet in reddish-brown on blued paper watermarked large crown.

Colour. Usually chocolate-brown on fairly deeply blued paper in the early printings, becoming a normal red-brown on slightly blued paper later. The plate was used for the transitional shades of pale red, orange and orange-brown on slightly blued paper: also for the pale red and pale rose shades on toned paper. It was kept in use during the period July 1857 when rose-red shades made their appearance, but this printing must have been exceedingly small as up-to-date fewer than a dozen copies has been seen in rose-red on white paper.

Watermark and Perforation. Always Large Crown. Perforation 14.

Check Letters. Conform to Alphabet III (*b*).

Notes. This plate also wore badly, but in this case an effort was made to remedy by hand serious defects occurring on AA, BA and TA.

AA	Two states: second state repair by hand retouch
BA	Two states: second state repair by hand retouch
BB	Second B defective in lower loop
BC	Margin weak over GE of POST-AGE

JA	Horizontal scratch through A and right side of square

KC	Fresh entry all squares, POST-AGE, value and margin below

KJ	Scratch across top of K square except in early printings

NJ	Tiny dot attached to left leg of N

NK	Mark below upper right serif of K

RK	K double below

SK	K double at foot of upright; more evident than in Plate 40
SL	Top line weak
TA	Two states: second state repair by hand retouch

PLATE 34   91

PLATE 34

Summary. Put to press 22.1.56; taken from press 25.3.62; defaced 1.12.64; sheets printed 724,100, of which about 100,000 were on blued paper; Imprimatur sheet in rich red chocolate-brown on slightly blued paper, watermarked large crown.

Colour. The first printings were in red-brown on blued paper which varied in depth from very deep red-brown to pale red-brown. Orange on blued paper occurs and is very scarce but orange-brown on blued paper is more frequent. In January 1857 the transitional shades on creamy and yellowish paper appeared followed by the same shades on white paper in March. Rose-red appeared on white paper in July and continued till the plate was withdrawn.

Watermark. Large Crown. *Perforation* usually 14 but the 16 gauge was temporarily used in late December 1857 and January to March 1858.

Check Letters. Alphabet III (*b*).

Notes. The alignment of the plate is fairly good; but IK–IL, JK–JL, KK–KL, LK–LL and MK–ML are very close together.

The N.E. square is strong but the right side tends to be weak. The base line of the S.E. square is generally weak and this became more marked when printings in rose-red began. This characteristic enables many stamps from this plate to be recognised with some degree of certainty. Mint blocks exist.

Very few dated copies are seen later than May 1862.

AH   Short vertical stroke in N.E. corner of H square

EB   Mark in left segment of N.E. square

DE   Tiny dot after toe of E

EC   Foot of E of POSTAGE obscured by blot

DF   Large smudge below N.E. square

EG   Dot after toe of E

EK   Lower right serif of K extends to right; right side extends above

FA   Mark on crown

FI   Short vertical scratch attached to N.W. corner of I square

GC   C lightly struck

GD   D hand cut and enlarged

GH   Short vertical scratch connects lower left serif of H to base line

GK   Slight evidence of double G at back

HH   Marks above and below left hand upright of second H

IC   Mark attached to right side above C square

JD   Base of D weak

KB   Different punch for K used (as on Plate 32)

KC   Slight burr line in right margin

KH   Outer side line of H square curved

LD   L very high

LE   Slight burr rub TAGE

LF   Large dot to right of top right serif of L

LG   L very high

MJ   Coincident fresh entry; J hand cut and enlarged slightly; spot on base of neck, in transitional and rose-red prints; burr line in both side margins

NH   Top right serif of H prolonged to right

OB   Coincident fresh entry; B faint

OD   D lightly struck

PB   Top line extends slightly on right (to distinguish it from Plate 37 PB)

PF   Dot to left of upper serif of P

QA   Scratch across A square from N.W. to S.E. in rose-red shades

RB   Long bottom serif to R

PLATE 34 93

SA	Blurred dot below S.E. corner of A square (to distinguish it from Plate 29 in blue paper copies)	SL	Dot after top right serif of L

		TE	Dot to right of lower right serif of T
SJ	Bottom line weak		

PLATE 35

Summary. Put to press 23.1.1856; defaced 22.6.1857; sheets printed 145,000; Imprimatur sheet in reddish-brown on blued paper watermarked large crown.

Colour. Normally red-brown on deeply blued paper in the early printings, becoming a paler red-brown on blued paper later. This plate took up the ink well, resulting in the stamps having a heavily inked appearance. Orange-brown shades occurred on blued paper, and later gave way to the transitional shades of pale red and pale rose on slightly blued paper, and finally to pale red and pale rose on toned paper. The plate was destroyed before the rose-red printings started.

Watermark and Perforation. Large Crown, perforated 14.

Check Letters. Alphabet III (*b*).

		ME	Blur above M
		MH	Top right serif of M extends to right
BI	I double		
		NE	Dot attached to toe of E
		OI	Blur to left of foot of I
		OL	Top line weak
KE	E handcut and misshapen	PA	Small horizontal scratches at base of P square
		PL	Top line weak
		RI	Small blur within foot of R
LD	L double		
LL	Dot in top of P of PENNY; margin weak over TAGE	SL	Vertical scratch in N.W. corner of S square

PLATE 36

Summary. Put to press 20.2.56; defaced, date unknown; withdrawn 1.3.64; sheets printed 1,004,900, of which about 100,000 were in red-brown on blued paper; Imprimatur sheet in rich chocolate-brown on paper considerably blued, watermarked large crown.

Watermark. Large Crown; *Perforation* 14. The 16 gauge temporarily used in late December 1857 and January to March 1858.

Colour. Printings from this plate are almost invariably in a deep colour, as though the plate took up a larger quantity of ink than normal. Deep chocolate colours on blued paper appeared at first, followed by a deep orange-brown and red-brown, until transitional shades appeared in January 1857. Pale rose and pale red shades are seen in March until rose-red appeared in July. This is nearly always a deep rich rose-red, nearly approaching a red-brown colour at times.

Check Letters. Alphabet III (*b*).

Notes. The plate was still in existence in 1872 as it was the original intention of Perkins Bacon to print a sheet in black for the Exhibition at South Kensington; Plate 27 however was selected.

The alignment of the plate is good. The N.E. square is strong and right side firm.

Mint blocks exist.

BF   Left side weak; thickened up-right to B

BK   Mark in and above GE in late printings

CK   Small dot on top margin to right of E

DA   A circular blur developed in right side of A square in 1858; it faded and disappeared in 1863

DC   Mark to left of D

DG   Right side extends slightly above

DK   Dot after lower right serif of K

GH   Short vertical scratch attached to N.W. corner of H square

GK   Dot in top of check letter G

JB   Mark on back of neck

PLATE 36   95

JJ   Mark in base of O of POSTAGE

JL   Horizontal scratch through N.W. square

LA   Large dot in margin above E

LB   Blot on sixth inner curved white line on left side

LI   Dot above lower left serif of L

MC   Right side extends slightly above

MH   Top right serif of H extends to right

NA   Large dot below E of PENNY

NF   Bottom line extends slightly on left

NK   Bottom line extends on left

OA   Top line extends on right

OD   Dot below S.E. corner of D square

PG   Big dot in upright of P of POSTAGE

PI   Large coloured dot in upper right half of O of ONE

QB   Upper serif of B prolonged

RC   Extremely like RC in Plate 31; the feet of R are of equal length in Plate 34, unequal in Plate 31

RH   Bottom line extends on left

TB   Horizontal guide line through T square and O

TC   Dot in front of centre of T; a scratch appeared in the right margin about December 1857

PLATE 37

Summary. Put to press 19.4.1856; defaced 29.10.1861; sheets printed 263,600; Imprimatur sheet in reddish-brown on blued paper water-marked large crown.

Colour. Normally deep red-brown on blued paper, becoming red-brown on blued paper in later printings. Subsequently orange-brown and orange-red shades occurred on blued paper, to be followed by the transitional shades of orange, pale red and pale rose on slightly blued paper. Pale red and pale rose next appeared on toned paper, and the plate was used for the July 1857 printings in rose-red on white paper.

Watermark, Large Crown. *Perforation* 14 on all blued paper and transitional shades, and most rose-red shades. The plate was still in use early in 1858 since sheets were issued perforated 16; these are scarce.

Check Letters. These conform to Alphabet III (*b*), but the M changes on this plate, for MA–MI have the wide M and MJ–ML the narrow one.

Note. The plate can have been little used for the rose-red printings as examples are uncommon.

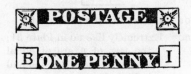

BI　　Marked fresh entry

BL　　L double below upright

DA　　Dot in T and dots under NN

DK　　Right side extends above

EA　　Dot over T

FI　　F very high

GB　　Short vertical stroke attached to N.W. corner of B square

HK　　Vertical stroke attached to N.W. corner of H square

KC　　Short horizontal stroke under K

KD　　Right lower serif of K double

KH　　Blurred dot below left leg of H, near base line; K fairly close to right side (*cf* Plate 45)

KK　　Vertical stroke attached to top line of second K square, very near to N.E. corner

LD　　Spots on left side of L square

LF　　Blurred dot above toe of L

LL　　Dot attached to toe of first L

ME　　Top right serif of M extends to right

MH　　Faint horizontal line in bottom of H square; bottom line extends to right

NB　　B slightly double below

PLATE 37   97

NC Top serifs of N prolonged slightly to left and right

NI Top right serif of I extends to right

NK K extremely close to left side of square

OG Large dot within G

OK N.E. square very weak, especially on right

PJ P very high

PL Blur in upper part of loop of P of PENNY (also on QL, RL and SL)

QD Blurred mark in N.W. corner of D square

RI I very close to left side of square

RL Dot in upper part of P of POSTAGE

SB B double above

SC C slightly thin

PLATE 38

Summary. Put to press 24.5.1856; defaced 29.10.1861; sheets printed 220,000; Imprimatur sheet in reddish-brown on blued paper watermarked large crown.

Colour. Normally red-brown on blued paper in the earliest printings, becoming a paler red-brown later on. Orange-brown and orange-red also occur on this plate, and the ink is sometimes so weak as to make the plating of the stamps difficult. They have nevertheless an attractive appearance.

Later transitional shades of pale red, pale rose and orange-red appeared on slightly blued paper, to be followed by pale red, orange and pale rose on toned paper. The plate was still in use in July 1857 when printing in rose-red began, and also early in 1858. Copies are uncommon however so that it was not used extensively.

Watermark, Large Crown; *Perforation* 14, except that copies printed in 1858 can be seen with perforation 16.

Check Letters. Alphabet III (c).

Note. There is a good example of a 'repair by hand' retouch on TB, the lateral borders of which had become worn.

G

BA	B rather large and square
BC	Upper curve of c very slightly double
BL	Bottom line extends on right
KJ	Blurred mark attached to top of square above upright of K
OA	Left lower corner of A square thickened
OG	Short vertical scratch in top of letter o

PJ	Foot of J slightly double

PL	Vertical scratch in left side of o of ONE

QK	Thick vertical scratch joins upright of K to top of square
TB	Two states; second state is repair by hand retouch
TD	Bottom line very weak

PLATE 39

Summary. Put to press 7.4.1856; defaced, date unknown; withdrawn 1.3.1864; sheets printed not known, but estimated at 110,000; Imprimatur sheet in rich chocolate-brown on slightly blued paper watermarked large crown.

Colour. The plate was used in 1861, 1862 and 1863. Impressions only appear in the paler shades of rose which were so frequent during those years; rose-pink describes the colour admirably. True rose-red or deep rose-red shades do not exist. The colour often is very pale and has a washed out appearance, and this has undoubtedly caused many specimens to be cast aside as 'shop-window shades'.

Watermark and Perforation. Large Crown, perforated 14.

Check Letters. Alphabet III (c).

Notes. This plate must have been placed in reserve for some years although the records state it was put to press in April, 1856. Examples on blued paper do not exist and no copy has yet been identified bearing a date in 1860. The majority of copies bear dates of 1862 and 1863.

    The alignment is very accurate. Mint blocks exist.

BG	Right side extends below
CH	Right side extends above considerably

DD	Large smudge through os

PLATE **39**

99

DG Large dot in margin below left foot of N of ONE

DK Right side extends above

EF Horizontal line above F, probably double letter

EJ Left side extends slightly below

FA One large blot on top line of N.E. square and a small smear at left side of same square

FG Spot on top of neck in front; G hand cut and much enlarged

GE Dot after top of G

GG Coincident fresh entry; both G's hand cut and much enlarged; several spots on chin and face and large dot near central dot in N.W. square; several small dots and scratches in N.E. square

GH Vertical scratch connects upper right serif of H to top of square

GJ Left side extends below

GK Letter G nearly touches right of square

ID Right side extends slightly below

IF Dot above bottom left serif of F

JH Short vertical scratch attached to N.W. corner of H square

KB Vertical blur in front of B

KL Top margin weak

MC Dot in S.W. corner of M square; M high central

OC Base of C double

PC Bottom line extends slightly on right

PL Dot to right of foot of P

QA   Dot below S.E. corner of A square

QH   Right side extends slightly below

RC   Dot on bottom of loop of O of ONE towards right

RH   Short vertical line in N.W. corner of H square

RI   Small blurred mark after curve of R

RJ   Spot on tip of bust

SC   Spot on forehead and scratch on bridge of nose

SD   Vertical scratch in N.W. corner of S square

SK   Two dots to left of s

TC   Top line extends on right

TH   Vertical scratch in N.W. corner of H square

TI   N.E. square recut by hand; bottom line extends on left

TK   Large dot beneath upper right major ray in N.W. square

TL   Heavy blot runs through lower portion of O of ONE extending into bottom margin

PLATE 40

Summary. Put to press 3.5.1856; defaced 22.6.1857; sheets printed 110,000; Imprimatur sheet in reddish-brown on blued paper water-marked large crown.

Colour. Normally a moderate red-brown on blued paper, but this soon gave way to many glorious shades of orange, bright and dark, orange-

PLATE 40   **101**

brown and pale orange-brown on deeply blued, moderately blued, and paper only slightly blued. These shades are most attractive and are practically confined to this plate.

In the pale orange on deeply blued paper the lettering is sometimes difficult to see if partially obscured by the cancellation, and plating is often made uncertain. A few shades appeared in pale red and pale rose on blued paper, but these are scarce.

Watermark and Perforation. Large Crown, perforated 14.

Check Letters. Alphabet III (c).

Note. The N.E. square is generally weak, particularly in later printings.

KJ   Foot of K slightly double

BF   Large blot across bottom of ear; F double

LD   L double

LJ   Large dot attached to centre of base lines at L square

HD   Fresh entry upper squares, POSTAGE and value

LL   Second L double below

KD   Left foot of K slightly double

MC   Short horizontal stroke below C square

KE   Left foot of K double

KH   Left foot of K slightly double   ME   Large spot on front of chest

MJ   Vertical thick scratch in base of E of POSTAGE

MK   Roll over M square and under O of ONE; right side extends slightly above

PH   Vertical scratch in N.W. corner of H square

PJ   Blur outside S.W. corner of J square

QG   Blurred mark at base of N.E. square

ML   Large dot in S.E. corner of M square; M double above

NC   N.E. square very weak

SK   K double at foot of upright, not so evident as in Plate 33

NH   Vertical scratch in left side of H square

TH   Tiny dot attached to base line of H square below centre of H; not evident in late printings

PLATE 41

Summary. Put to press 7.4.1856; defaced, date unknown; withdrawn 7.3.1864; sheets printed 361,609; Imprimatur sheet in rich chocolate-brown on paper watermarked large crown which showed marked blueing.

Notes. Although the date given for going to press is 7.4.1856, this is exceedingly unlikely as no impressions have been found on blued paper or even in transitional shades; indeed copies do not make their appearance until June, 1861. It is stated in Sir Edward Bacon's book that this plate was repaired, but he gives no details as to the nature or the time when this was carried out.

After examination of used and mint examples it has been found that this repair consisted of re-entering the top four horizontal rows with a few exceptions, also many of the check letters were recut by hand and in some cases their position was altered. All copies are in the repaired state. The re-entering on the top four vertical rows was coincident in every case.

The watermark is always Large Crown, perforated 14; the colour is rose-red on white paper.

This plate has a characteristic N.E. square in which the top line and

PLATE 41   103

often the side line are very thin. The one o'clock major ray is always
weak. This obtains on every stamp except in those subjected to repair
by re-entry.

The plate is somewhat scarcer than the total printing would suggest.
The Check Letters are Alphabet III (*b*).

AA No evidence of repair; N.E.
square and right side weak

AB Re-entered; N.E. square and
right side strong

AC Re-entered; N.E. square and
right side strong; burr rub
value; N.E. joined; mark on
bust

AD Re-entered; N.E. square and
right side strong

AE Re-entered; N.E. square and
right side strong

AF No evidence of repair; N.E.
square and right side very
weak

AG Re-entered; N.E. square and
right side strong; G hand cut
and misshapen; short vertical stroke in N.W. corner of
A square

AH Re-entered; N.E. square and
right side strong

AI Re-entered; N.E. square and
right side strong

AJ Re-entered; N.E. square
strong; right side fairly
strong; burr line in left
margin

AK Re-entered; N.E. square
strong; right side fairly
strong

AL No evidence of repair; N.E.
square weak; right side
fairly strong

BA Re-entered; N.E. square
strong; right side fairly
strong; B hand cut

BB Re-entered; N.E. square
strong; right side fairly
strong; first B only hand cut

BC Re-entered; N.E. square
strong; right side fairly
strong; B hand cut

BD Re-entered; N.E. square
strong; right side fairly
strong; B hand cut; spot on
base of bust

BE Re-entered; N.E. square
strong; right side fairly
strong; both letters hand cut

BF Re-entered; N.E. square
strong but right side still
weak with strong burr line;
both letters hand cut and
position of F altered

-BG Re-entered; N.E. square and
right side strong; both letters hand cut and position of
G altered

BH Re-entered; N.E. square and
right side strong; B hand cut

BI Re-entered; N.E. square and
right side strong; B hand cut
with dot in front of lower
serif

BJ Re-entered; N.E. square and
right side strong; B hand cut

BK Re-entered; N.E. square and
right side strong; B hand cut

BL Re-entered; N.E. square and
right side strong; B hand cut
and position altered

CA–CJ Re-entered; N.E. square strong; right side fairly strong

OJ Mark on back of neck

CK Re-entered; N.E. square strong; right side fairly strong; blur attached to top of K

PC Marks in N.E. square

CL No evidence of repair; N.E. square weak; right side fairly strong

QJ Blur in N.E. corner of J square

DA–DL Re-entered; N.E. square strong; right side fairly strong

QL Distinct mark on margin below E P

SD Vertical scratch in outer quadrant of N.W. square

EI Short vertical stroke in S.E. corner of N.W. square

SE Blurred mark below and to left of S

FE Small scratch in S.E. corner of F square

SF Two small scratches over F

FF Thick scratch parallel to 7 o'clock major ray in N.W. square

TB Top line of N.E. square extremely weak

JJ Dot in margin some way below S.E. corner of first J square

TD Vertical scratch in S.W. corner of T square and extends outside square

LE Side line of N.E. square nearly absent and top line of N.E. square very weak

MD Slanting scratch in base of M square

TG Scratch through lower right portion of O of POSTAGE

ME Dot in S.W. corner of M square

PLATE 41   105

TH   Blurred mark on base line of T square to left of T; tiny dot in margin above E towards its right

TJ   Dot in middle of S of POSTAGE

PLATE 42

Summary. Put to press 7.4.1856; taken from press 29.1.1862; defaced 1.12.1864; sheets printed 669,700, of which about 100,000 were on blued paper; Imprimatur sheet in rich chocolate-brown on paper which showed marked blueing, watermarked large crown.

Notes. The earliest shades are in red-brown on blued paper and an orange-brown made its appearance in early 1857. The transitional shades on toned paper followed to give way to the final rose-red shade which persisted until 1864.

The Queen's head is generally rather weak and this gave rise to the cameo appearance. Many beautiful shades and copies come from this plate.

The Watermark is Large Crown and Perforation 14. The plate was however used for the temporary perforation 16 issue of December 1857 to March 1858.

A repair was done on TC and TD. The reason is hard to find as these impressions were satisfactory. The re-entry was coincident with the original but the check letters became thinned. Rose-red impressions are always in the repaired state, whilst those on blued paper are in the original state. The N.E. square is generally weak.

Mint blocks exist.

The Check Letters are Alphabet III (*c*).

AA   Well marked fresh entry upper squares, POSTAGE and value

AI   Very heavy blur right side of I square

BF   Top line extends on right

AC   Vertical scratch on hair runs into jewel

BG   Serif of G lengthened

BH   Vertical scratch across face

BJ   Right side extends below

CK   Large spot on face opposite nostril

FA   Dot outside N.E. corner of N.E. square

FG   Blur through GE in rose-red shades

HL   H well to right side of square

IH   Lower right serif of H double

IK   Bottom line extends on left

JJ   Bottom line extends on left

KA   Dot in N.E. corner of A square

LF   Mark on left margin opposite eye

LH   Lower left portion of L double

MA   Short coloured stroke attached to top of A

MG   Dot in S.W. corner of M square

MI   Large dot almost attached to lower left serif of M

ML   Large dot in S.E. corner of M square

NB   Tiny stroke attached to lower loop of B

OB   Vertical scratch through B in late impressions

OE   Top line extends on right

PF   P nearly touches right side of square

QL   Second state: repair by hand retouch

RA   Top line extends on right

RD   Right side extends slightly above

SD   Short horizontal scratch in S.E. corner of S square

PLATE 42 107

SH Base of s filled with blur mark

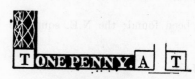

TA Horizontal scratch from S.E. corner of A square runs under T of TB; only seen on blue paper and in transitional shades and in early impressions in rose-red shades; several dots in margin under NNY and in value; these dots are not seen on very early impressions on blue paper; large dot on left margin opposite base of neck in rose-red shades

TB Horizontal line beneath T square (see TA); spot on nose and spot behind mouth occurs at different times in late printings

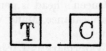

TC Two states; first state normal; second state coincident re-entry; both letters faint

TD Two states; first state normal; second state coincident re-entry; both letters faint; horizontal line through Y and full stop close to base line of D square

TF Top line extends on right; upper bar of F weak in centre

TJ Full stop partially obliterated; blurred dot attached to left side of J square opposite ball of J

TL L double at foot

PLATE 43

Summary. Put to press 5.7.1856; defaced, date unknown; withdrawn 2.4.1864; sheets printed, not known, but must have been nearly one million or slightly more; probably 125,000 were on blued paper; Imprimatur sheet in red-brown on paper which is slightly blued watermarked large crown.

Notes. The earliest shades are in red-brown on blued paper; orange-brown appeared in early 1857. Transitional shades on toned paper followed to give way to the final rose-red shade which persisted until 1864.

The Queen's head is generally very weak and this gives rise to the cameo appearance. Many very beautiful shades and copies come from this plate.

The Watermark is Large Crown and Perforation 14. The plate was however used for the temporary perforation 16 issue of December 1857 to March 1858.

No evidence of plate repair has been found; the N.E. square is generally weak and often very weak.

Mint blocks exist.

The Check Letters are Alphabet III (*c*).

AC   Dot within c and mark in front of A

AG   Spot on cheek

BB   Marks over POSTAGE

BF   Top line extends on right; tiny scratch in S.E. corner of B square; spot on angle of jaw

CF   Blur mark at base of third jewel in early rose-red printings

DG   Mark in N.W. corner of G square in rose-red shades

DI   Tiny dot after middle of D in late printings

DJ   Mark over E of POSTAGE

DL   Thin oblique scratch connects base of L to base line

EB   Several marks after top of E

EH   Vertical stroke connects left leg of H to base line

EI   Short vertical stroke under letter E

EK   Dot attached to top of upright of K

PLATE 43 109

FE Dot in front of E

GB Mark in margin below NN

IK Lower right serif of I extends to right

JD Very like JD Plate 44; there is a small blurred mark after J on Plate 43

KE Left foot of K double

LI Vertical mark attaches lower left serif of L to base line

LJ L double below

LL Blurred mark below and attached to upright of first L; vertical curved dotted line extending entire length of left side of second L square

MD Vertical scratch in N.W. corner of D square

ML Tiny dot in S.W. corner of M square

NB Top line extends on right

NC Right side extends slightly above

NG Dot under left foot of N

OA Small blurred A

PA Dot below left leg of A in rose-red shades only

PI Blurred mark on upper half of P of POSTAGE in rose-red shades

PJ Small dot in front of J

QC Coloured dot in centre of P of PENNY

QG Bottom line extends on left

QK Horizontal scratch beneath lower right serif of K in rose-red shades

QL Many dots N.W. of L in rose-red shades

RC   Fresh entry value

RE   Break in top of R develops in late printings

RJ   Fresh entry N.W. square and POSTAGE; dot attached to base of J

RL   L weak; several smudgy marks in upper part of L square

TH   Horizontal scratch through base of PENNY and H square

TJ   Blur in upper part of back of G

TK   Lower serif of K beneath upright is distinctly double; the other lower serif is slightly double

TL   Mark below NY in nearly all rose-red printings; does not occur on blue paper or transitional shades; bottom line extends slightly on right

PLATE 44

Summary. Put to press 19.7.1856; taken from press 20.4.1861; defaced 29.10.1861; sheets printed 601,500, of which about 100,000 were on blued paper; Imprimatur sheet in a rich chocolate colour on paper slightly blued watermarked large crown.

Notes. The earliest shades are in red-brown on blued paper, and orange-brown may be found in early 1857. Transitional shades on toned paper followed to give way to the final rose-red shade which persisted until 1864.

The Watermark is Large Crown and Perforation 14. The plate was used, however, for the temporary perforation 16 issue of December 1857 to March 1858. Strangely the watermark is found inverted on this plate not infrequently. The N.E. square is always weak. No evidence of plate repair has been found.

Mint blocks exist.

The Check Letters are Alphabet III (*c*).

PLATE 44   111

AB   A thick line extends obliquely into margin below from N of ONE

AC   Mark on crown on late impressions

AD   Left side extends below

BA   Base line weak

BB   Burr line upper third of left side

CD   Dot over C nearly touching top margin

CE   Vertical scratch under C

CG   Bottom line extends on right

CH   Mark within C and bottom line extends slightly on right

CI   Horizontal line and dot below C square

EB   Lower quarter of left side cut by hand

FE   Lower serif of E extends to left

FK   F close to left side of square

FL   Dot in S.W. corner of L square

GA   Top line extends slightly on right

GK   Serif of G lengthened both ends

HB   Dot below S.E. corner of B square

HE   Top line extends slightly on right

HF   Top line extends slightly on right

ID   Right side extends slightly below

JD   Very like JD of Plate 43; no mark after J (see Plate 43); scratch across N.E. square in late impressions

JI   Bottom line extends slightly on right

KI   I very high to right

LA   Top line extends slightly on right

MA   Coloured dot in extreme N.E. corner of N.E. square; top line extends on right

MF   Dot attached to left bottom serif of M, and dot attached to bottom margin; dot above top left serif of F

MH   Large dot in S.W. corner of M square

MI   M double above

MK   Dot in S.W. corner of M square

NB   Right side extends below

NH   Top line extends on right

NI   Top right serif of I extended to right

NJ   Top right serif of N extended to left

NL   Margin weak over GE

OC   Very like Plate 46; no frame extensions

OD   Top line extends slightly on right

OI   I very high to left

PH   Right side extends slightly below

PK   Left bottom serif of K slightly double

QC   Spot on nostril in transitional and rose-red shades

QG   Bottom line extends slightly on left

QH   Very faint vertical line in right side of N.E. square

RC   Mark in N.W. square in rose-red shades

RD   Top line extends slightly on right

RH   Tiny dot in margin above and to left of O of POSTAGE

RJ   Ball of foot of J double

RK   Scratch on face in late impressions

SB   Dot in S.E. corner of S square

SD   Large spot on collar bone in late rose-red prints

SE   Bottom line weak

PLATE 44   113

SF   Bottom line extends on right

TA   Horizontal scratch in N.E. corner of T square in late copies

TH   Large dot in top of A of POSTAGE and tiny scratch above left upright of H

TJ   Top and bottom lines extend on right

PLATE 45

Summary. Put to press 26.8.1856; defaced 29.10.1861; sheets printed 111,000; Imprimatur sheet in dull rose-red on very slightly blued paper watermarked large crown.

Notes. The colour is normally red-brown on blued paper; shades of orange-brown appeared later on paper less blued. Subsequently transitional shades of pale red and pale rose appeared on paper slightly blued, to be followed by these shades on toned paper. The latter are scarce since this plate was evidently not much used until its withdrawal in 1861.

Copies appeared in rose-red on white paper but these are scarce: this issue also appeared with the perforation 16 of December 1857 to March 1858. These are rare and few specimens are seen.

The lettering conforms to Alphabet III (*c*) and the perforation is 14 except for the 16 gauge already mentioned.

BJ   Blur before top of B

CF   Horizontal line through full stop and S.W. corner of F square

FJ   Dot above J

GD   Two thick spots in E. segment of N.E. square; vertical stroke in T of POSTAGE; vertical gash on hair

HC   Marks in top and bottom of Y of PENNY, attached to side of C square

KD   Lower left serif of K double

H

KH   Horizontal blurred scratch below left leg of H near base line; K centred (*cf* Plate 40)

LB   Vertical scratches beneath leg of B and to left

LD   L double below

LH   Dot attached to base line beneath left leg of H

LI   L double below

MI   Blur on base of I

MJ   Spot on tip of bust in very late printings

NC   Vertical scratch in E. segment of N.W. square; scratches in O of POSTAGE in late printings only

ND   Tiny mark within D

OC   Tiny dot in top of letter O

OI   Base of I slightly double

OL   O very high

PH   Left foot of H double

QC   Blurred dot within C

QH   Thick line through top of head

RE   Heavy blurred circular mark before E, and slightly before R

RF   Spot in middle of cheek to right of nostril; top margin weak over GE

RH   R very high; blur above left serif of H

RK   R very high

SA   Bottom line weak below E of PENNY

SB   Top line weak

SG   Spot on cheek behind mouth

TA   Dots in top of NY

TB   Mark in bottom of E of POST-AGE in later printings

TE   Marks in NNY

TI   Large dot between upper right serif of T and right side of square

PLATE 46   115

PLATE 46

Summary. Put to press 27.8.1856; taken from press 28.4.1862; defaced 1.12.1864; sheets printed 651,400, of which about 80,000 were on blued paper; Imprimatur sheet in red-brown on slightly blued paper water-marked large crown.

Notes. The earliest shades are in red-brown on blued paper. Beautiful orange-brown shades occurred in early 1857 followed by transitional shades on toned paper. Rose-red appeared on white paper in July and persisted throughout the remainder of the plate's life.

The Watermark is Large Crown and Perforation 14. The plate was used however for the temporary perforation 16 issue of December 1857 to March 1858.

The impressions generally are rather weak, the stamps having a worn appearance. A brick-red colour which occurs frequently is almost con-fined to this plate. The N.E. square is weak. Mint blocks exist. No evidence of plate repair has been found.

The Check Letters are Alphabet III (*c*) except that PJ, PK, PL have a narrow looped P belonging to Alphabet III (*d*).

BH Fresh entry upper squares of POSTAGE and in margin below (see CH)

BK Marks in right side of N.E. square

CH Marks in margin above from BH fresh entry

EL L very high to right

FI Mark in foot of first N of PENNY

GE G double

GI Spot on tip of nose and on cheek; dot on S.W. corner of I square; G hand cut and marks in G square

HA Short horizontal scratch below P of PENNY

HC Marks in top of NY; C close to right side of square

HD Mis-shaped D to right

HI Fresh entry upper squares

LI Fresh entry upper squares

LK K extremely close to left side of square which is curved

MA Right side extends slightly above

MC Small dot in S.W. corner of M square

MH Large dot almost touches bottom line of H square to left of H

MI N.E. square very weak and markedly so in late impressions; top line weak over GE; burr rub from LI fresh entry

ML Tiny dot near S.E. corner of M square

NA Marks in N.E. square in rose-red prints

NL Bottom line extends on right

OC Very like OC Plate 44; top line extends on right

OD Mis-shaped O to left

OJ Vertical scratch parallel to left side of O square and adjacent to it within

OL Dot in S.W. corner of L square

PA Dot in lower left portion of O of POSTAGE

PG Tiny dot in front of letter P, more evident in later prints

PI P nearly touches right side of square

QB Two blurred dots below up-right of E of ONE

PLATE 46 117

RD Top line extends on right

SL Dot in lateral segment of N.E. square

TA Three dots above N.W. square

TB Top line extends on right

TH Short vertical scratch in N.W. corner of H square close to side of square

PLATE 47

Summary. Put to press 15.12.1856; withdrawn 30.3.1864; sheets printed 953,900, of which a small quantity were on blued paper, possibly not more than 30,000; Imprimatur sheet in red-brown on slightly blued paper watermarked large crown.

Notes. The earliest shades are in red-brown and orange-brown on deeply blued paper. These were followed by transitional shades on toned paper. Rose-red appeared on white paper in July and persisted till the plate was withdrawn.

The Watermark is Large Crown and Perforation 14. The plate was used however for the temporary perforation 16 issue of December 1857 to March 1858.

The impressions are stronger than on Plate 46 but the N.E. square is still weak. Large mint blocks are known. No repair to this plate has been discovered.

The Check Letters are Alphabet III (*d*).

AA Vertical line close to and outside left side of first A square

AG Several marks in G square

AB Letter B hand cut and enlarged

AH H double below

AE Top line extends on right; small dot attached to toe of E

AI Vertical scratch in left fork of Y

AL Large spot in Y in late prints

BD   Dot on margin above left corner of N.E. square

BE   Mark attached to back of E

BF   Tiny mark close to margin below B

BG   Tiny dot below serif of G

CC   Right side extends above

DC   Mark in top of P of PENNY

DI   Mark above back of D

DL   Left side extends slightly below

EC   Top of curve of C double; dot to right of toe of E

HA   Lines of N.E. square cross

HG   Blur in top of H

IA   Small dot after I about two-thirds way down

IF   Vertical scratch runs near and parallel to left side of F square; dot after lower left serif of F

JH   Short vertical scratch attached close to N.W. corner of H square

JL   Bottom line extends slightly on left

KB   Different punch used for B; B is of later type seen on Plate 52 and following plates

KF   Left side extends slightly below

LF   Short vertical scratch attached to base line of F square close to S.W. corner

LH   Left foot of H double

LI   Short mark attached to left side of L below upper left serif

LL   Short vertical stroke in front of top portion of first L

PLATE 47   119

MG   Different roller used; N.E. square strong; G hand cut and considerably enlarged

· NH   H touches right side of square

NK   Top right serif of K extends to side of square

OF   Bottom line extends slightly on left

OJ   Left side extends below

PG   Dot attached to base of P

QA   Several marks in POSTAGE; top line extends on right

QB   Right side extends above

QF   Top and bottom lines extend on left

RG   Scratch on bridge of nose; not present on early prints in rose-red

RH   Mark on bottom margin below left foot of H; bottom line extends on left

RK   Dot on tip of bust; R hand cut with enlarged loop and long bottom serif; dot in E of PENNY in early printings only

RL   Several marks around L

SJ   Mark in back of G of POSTAGE

TB   Margin weak over GE

PLATE 48

Summary. Put to press 2.2.1857; withdrawn 1.3.1864; sheets printed not known, but a total of at least 800,000 is likely, of which a minute number, probably not exceeding 1000, were on blued paper; Imprimatur sheet is in red-brown on slightly blued paper watermarked large crown.

Notes. The earliest shades were in red-brown on blued paper and specimens in this state are exceedingly rare. Transitional shades on toned paper followed and rose-red on white paper appeared in July. This persisted until the plate was withdrawn. A paler shade of rose-red is commonly found on this plate prior to 1862, when the rose-red shade generally became more of a rose-pink colour.

The Watermark is Large Crown and Perforation 14. The plate was used however for the temporary perforation 16 issue of December 1857 to March 1858.

The N.E. square is weak but the impressions are strong. QL and TL were repaired by hand and thus exist in two states. Mint blocks exist.

The Check Letters are Alphabet III (d).

AH   Right side extends above

AI   Large spot in top of P of POSTAGE

AL   L double at top

BB   Top line extends on right

BG   Fresh entry; both letters hand cut

BI   Small dot near tip of bust

DC   Oblique mark below NN (see EC)

DH   Short vertical stroke in N.W. corner of H square; D close to left side of square

EA   Right side extends slightly above

EC   N.E. square weak; mark in margin over GE

EH   Mark on base line below left leg of H

FA   Right side extends slightly above

FL   Short horizontal stroke above F

GD   G double

GL   L slightly double below

IC   Scratch attaches N.E. corner of N.E. square to S.W. corner of HC

JB   Bottom line extends slightly on left

JL   Foot of J hand cut, rounded and enlarged

KH   Two dots below right leg of H

KI   Bottom line extends slightly on right

PLATE 48   121

LD Bottom line extends slightly on right

LJ Large smudge at left side of J square and large spot behind mouth

MF Right bottom serif of M extends to side margin

NI Large dot on base of N.E. square

OA Large coloured mark in S.E. portion of N.E. square

OH Bottom line extends slightly on right

OI I very high; top line of square irregular

QA Top line extends on right

QB Top line extends on right

QC Blurred mark attached to back of C in early printings

QF Bottom line extends on left

QK Bottom line extends on left

QL Scratch beneath nostril in late prints; exists in two states, the second state is a repair by hand retouch

RD Blurred mark beneath upright of D

RH Short vertical stroke in N.W. corner of H square

RK Marks below S.W. corner of R square

SH S well to right side of square

TL Two states; second state is a repair by hand retouch; dot below and near corner of L square

PLATE 49

Summary. Put to press 3.4.1857; defaced 29.10.1861; sheets printed 473,200; Imprimatur sheet in red-brown on slightly blued paper watermarked large crown.

Notes. This is the first plate of Die II from which no examples exist on blued paper. The first printings were in a pale transitional shade of rose on toned paper. Few sheets could have been done on this shade and copies are scarce. The rose-red shade appeared in July. A pale shade of rose-red is usual.

This plate suffered very badly from the effects of corrosion. This is very marked on a large number of stamps in the lower half of the sheet. The vast majority of impressions show spots and blemishes and many occur in the gutter margins between the stamps. This may account for the early withdrawal of the plate in 1861. The N.E. square is stronger on this plate, indicating that a different roller was used.

The Watermark is Large Crown and Perforation 14. The plate was used for the temporary perforation 16 issue of December 1857 to March 1858; comparatively few sheets must have been so perforated as specimens are scarce. Very little exists in the way of mint blocks. No repair is known to have been undertaken.

The Check Letters are Alphabet III (d).

AC   Scratch in N.W. square; blur round c

AD   Fresh entry POSTAGE; marks in N.W. square and letter squares; both letters surrounded by blur marks

AE   Blur marks round both letters; left side very weak

AF   Blur marks round both letters

AH   Small dot to right of foot of H

BA   Large dot in lower part of N.E. square

BB   Mark above and to right of E in margin above; dot in toe of E of POSTAGE

BC   Dot in N.E. square at right side and dot above corner of N.E. square

BE   Blur marks round both letters; scratch in right margin

BF   Blur marks round both letters; top line extends on right

BG   Dot near top right corner of N.E. square; slight blurring in letter squares

BJ   Much out of alignment, hence stamps are usually badly off-centre

PLATE 49 123

BL   Small blur mark beneath L

CA   Blur round A and marks above corner of N.E. square

FL   Scratch extends back from lower left serif of L into full stop and Y

CB   Two dots in N.E. square

CC   Marks in N.E. square and outside it on right; blur marks round both letters

GA   Dot to right of G; dot in margin above and to left of P

CD   Blur marks round both letters

CE   Heavy blur round C

CF   Heavy blur round C

GB   Dot over E

⌁ CG   Heavy blur round both letters; dot in N.E. square

CH   Blur mark above C

GG   Small mark in lower portion of N.W. square

CL   C very low and close to right

HA   Dot on right side of N.E. square near top

DE   Dot attached to toe of E

HL   Scratch in right margin near top in early printings

DH   Short vertical stroke in N.W. corner of H square

EK   Dot in left side of O of POSTAGE

IB   Blur mark in left side of N.W. square

IE   Blur mark in left side of E square in early printings

EL   Dot after foot of L

JD   Marks in D square

FA   Dots in margin below ONE P

JL   Short vertical stroke in N.W. corner of L square

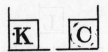

KC   Dot in front of K; blur in C square

KD   Horizontal scratches in margin below

KF   Strong blur mark below right foot of K

KG   Blur marks round letters

KJ   Blur mark above K

KK   Horizontal scratch after top right serif of first K

LA   Large dot after A

LB   Blur mark after top of B in early printings

LE   Strong dot in front of E; blur on toe of L

LG   Horizontal scratch through L; blur around G

LK   Two dots after top right serif of K close to side of square

MA   N.E. square very weak; tiny dot below S.E. corner of A square

MF   Dot near left side of M square

MG   Dot between M and bottom left corner of square

MI   M very high

ML   Scratch in right margin

NB   Dot below Y; two dots in letter G

NC   Several dots in N square; heavy blur round C

ND   Several dots and blur marks in lower margin; strong blur in front of D

NF   Thick scratch from lower right corner of N square extending below O of ONE

NJ   N high central

PLATE 49   125

OA Top line extends slightly on right

OB Large number of dots in right margin of N.E. square and a few in top margin

OC Large number of marks in value, letter squares and in lower margin

OD Large number of marks in value and lower margin very similar to OC; large dot in N.E. square

OG Right side very weak

OI Dot in right side of O of ONE

OL Vertical scratch close to upper part of right side; dot in top of letter O

PB Large number of dots in POSTAGE and N.E. square; some dots and blur marks on right side; large marks in B square and value; horizontal scratches and marks in lower margin

Q-C (Top)

PC Large number of dots in upper squares, POSTAGE, value and letter squares; also in top and bottom margins and right side; a few dots in the left margin

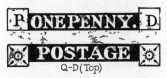

Q-D (Top)

PD Large number of dots in letter squares, value, lower margin, N.W. square and POSTAGE

PE Several large dots in P square and a few in value

QA Several dots in right margin

R-B (Top)

QB Large number of dots in upper squares, POSTAGE, letter squares, value and in all margins

R-C (Top)

QC Large number of dots in upper squares, POSTAGE, letter squares, value and in all margins

R–D (Top)

QD   Large number of dots in upper squares, POSTAGE, letter squares, value and in all margins

QF   Dot below Q

QK   Dot in upper right corner of N.E. square

RA   Large number of dots in right margin

RB   Large number of dots in right margin and value

RC   Large number of dots in right margin, POSTAGE, value and all squares

RD   Large number of dots in right margin, value and letter squares

RE   Marks in POSTAGE

RF   Dots in lower margin

RG   Dots in lower and upper margins

RI   R high to left

SB   Large number of dots upper and lower margins and value

SC   Blur on left side of C square

SD   Several indistinct dots in S square; dot in centre of D

SE   Large number of dots in upper squares, POSTAGE, lower squares and on all margins; generally weak

SF   Large number of dots in upper squares, POSTAGE, lower squares and on all margins; generally weak

SG   Several dots below S square

SH   Left network very weak; dot below corner of H square

SI   Base line weak

SK   Several dots in upper and lower margins

SL   Blur round base of L

TA   Mark in back of G

TC   Marks in all squares, POSTAGE, and value; generally weak

TD   Large number of dots in upper squares and POSTAGE

TE   Large number of dots in upper squares and POSTAGE

PLATE 49   127

TF Large number of dots in upper   TH Left network weak
    squares and POSTAGE;
    generally weak

TG Marks in upper margin; right
    network weak   TK Two dots in N.E. square

PLATE 52*

Summary. Put to press 7.5.1857; withdrawn, date unknown but probably 1.3.1864; sheets printed, not known but a printing of approximately 1,000,000 sheets is likely; Imprimatur sheet in light orange-red on white paper watermarked large crown.

Notes. The earliest printings were in a rose colour on toned paper, but specimens from these are very scarce. Rose-red appeared in July and persisted until the plate was withdrawn. As copies are plentiful with early 1864 dates the plate is not thought to have been withdrawn until the general withdrawal of 'Star plates' on 1.3.1864.

This plate suffered from the effects of corrosion, but not to such a degree as did Plate 49. Many stamps show unsightly marks and spots, very often in the letter squares. Many marks appear in the gutter margins.

The N.E. square and the right side are strong on this plate indicating the use of a fresh roller.

The Watermark is Large Crown and Perforation 14. The plate was used for the temporary perforation 16 issue of December 1857 to March 1858. Mint blocks exist. TA was repaired by hand and thus exists in two states.

The Check Letters are Alphabet III (*e*).

AK Left side line of A square
    covered in numbers of dots
    of varying sizes

AB Large vertical thick scratch in
    front of ear in late prints

AJ Several marks and large dot   BA Dots above POSTAGE and above
    around J   right foot of A

* For Plates 50 and 51 see Chapter Five.

BF　Blur within upper loop of B; blurred scratch to left of F

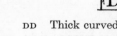

BG　Thick mark attached to back of G and marks in G square

BI　Tiny dot after I

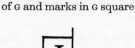

BJ　Smudged mark above N.E. square and marks within square

BK　Small linear mark under upright of B

CH　Mark in base of N.E. square

CJ　Marks above N.E. square

CK　Marks above GE and dot beneath upper left serif of K

DD　Thick curved blur in second D square

DH　Blurred mark in lower segment of N.E. square

DI　Burr rub in POSTAGE

DK　Dot attached to margin over S

EA　Dot attached to side of A square

EG　Dot above upper right serif of G

EH　Dot above upright of E

EK　Large dot to left of lower left serif of E

EL　Dot in N.W. corner of L square

FB　Dot attached to back of F

PLATE 52   129

FC Dot in margin opposite nose

GB Top line extends on right

GC Dot within base of letter G

GH Vertical line in left side of N.W. square

GJ Thick smudged line in N.E. square

HH Several marks in first H square

HJ Several marks in J square

HK Mark on neck

HL Mark below upright of L

IC Large dot attached to outside of S.W. corner of I square

IF Several marks in F square

I

IG Dot in top of G

IH Several marks in N.W. square

II Dot in right segment of N.E. square and mark after second I

IJ Several dots after I

JA Dot below right upright of N of ONE

JC Dot below left upright of N of ONE

JD Several dots in D square and on base line

JG Several marks in N.E. square and in margin over GE

JH Several marks in H square

JI Several marks in J square

JJ   Large dot above first J and many dots in left margin

JK   Mark attached to left side of J square

KI   Many dots on top margin and in N.W. square

KJ   Dot above lower left serif of K

KK   Blurred line to left of first K

LB   Scratch across forehead
LH   Dot below corner of H square

LJ   Several dots to left of J

LK   Several dots around L

MG   Left side extends below; several dots on G

MK   Small mark above M

NA   Two short scratches run horizontally across A square

NC   Several dots in square and another in base of Y

NF   Dot below foot of N and short scratch in top of square

NI   Dot after I
OE   Bottom line extends on right

OF   Scratch above N.W. square

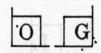

OG   Dot above and to left of O and dots outside G square

OH   Several marks within letter O

OI   Dot in top of O

PLATE 52 131

OJ   Dot in top of o

PE   Small blurred marks above E
      which is very high central;
      blurred dot near S.E. corner
      of P square

PF   Short horizontal scratch in S.E.
      corner of P square

PH   Short vertical line in N.W.
      corner of H square

QA–QL   Small blurred Q

QA   A slightly larger than normal

QC   C well to right side of square

QD   Several dots around blurred Q

QG   Dot in top of G

RF   Heavy blur mark in front of F

RG   Marks within G

RH   Fine straight scratch connects
      S.E. corner of H square with
      N.E. corner of N.E. square
      of SH

RI   R hand cut with lengthened
      tail and somewhat enlarged;
      probably converted from
      original P

RL   Blur round R and in top of T

SA   Dot in left side of O of ONE

SB   Horizontal short line between
      upright of B and base line;
      small dot below base line to
      left of this short line

SF   Two small marks to left of F

SL   Margin weak over TAGE

TA   Two states; second state is
      repair by hand retouch

TE   Several dots to left of E

TF   Large number of dots in value

TG   Several dots around T, G and
      marks in N.E. square

TK   Upper right arm and serif of K
      weak

PLATE 53

Summary. Put to press 12.2.1857; defaced 29.10.1861; sheets printed, not known but a printing of a very few sheets only is likely; Imprimatur sheet in red-brown on white paper watermarked large crown.

Notes. This plate is exceedingly rare and to date only three copies in used condition have been found, together with a mint portion of the upper five rows in rose-red.

Two of these copies are in a very pale shade of rose on toned paper, suggesting that the date of being put to press is accurate; the other copy is in a normal colour of rose-red.

Wright & Creeke in their *A History of the Adhesive Stamps of the British Isles* state: 'Stamps on right half of the sheet very irregularly spaced horizontally, others fairly regular. Plate condemned in consequence and withdrawn 29.10.1861.'

As the used specimens are so exceedingly rare this date of 1861 is interesting. Either the error in transferring was noticed early and the plate laid on one side early in 1858 and defaced three years later, or the total printings from this plate were destroyed, a few sheets being perforated experimentally to see if issue were possible.

No varieties have been detected.

The Check Letters are Alphabet III (*e*).

PLATE 55

Summary. Put to press 21.5.1857; withdrawn 1.3.1864; sheets printed not known, but a total of close on 1,000,000 sheets is likely; Imprimatur sheet in light orange-red on white paper watermarked large crown.

Notes. An extremely small first printing was made in rose on toned paper; copies are very rare. Rose-red appeared in July and persisted throughout the plate's life.

This plate is remarkable in that the entries A, B and C vertical rows were re-entered prior to the plate being registered. It is possible that some or all of the D vertical row were likewise repaired. The marks of re-entry are extremely similar on the sixty odd stamps affected. Many are well marked, others less so, whereas a few show only the slightest trace. The general character of the re-entry marks being so consistent suggests that these were conveyed by the roller. It has been previously thought that these marks were left after the three rows had been erased, which would have been an extremely difficult process, and remained after re-entry. It is difficult to support this view on the evidence. The re-entering was carried out before the check letters were inserted as these are not affected. The plate did not suffer from corrosion.

The N.E. square is strong; the right side is generally strong.

PLATE 55   133

The Watermark is Large Crown and Perforation 14. The plate was used for the temporary perforation 16 issue of December 1857 to March 1858.

Mint blocks exist and the plate is known completely reconstructed in mint condition. SL and TL were repaired by hand and thus exist in two states.

The Check Letters are Alphabet III (*f*).

AA   Re-entry (see above)

AF   Dot in N.E. square almost touching side line; bottom line extends on right

AG   Dot after G; right side blurred

AJ   Dot in front of A; another almost touching top of A

AK   Horizontal scratch in N of ONE

BA   Re-entry (see above)

BH   Dot in N.W. corner of H square

BK   Marks below Y (see CK)

BL   Tiny dot on toe of L

CA   Re-entry (see above)

CJ   Several dots over E

CK   Marks above GE (see BK)

CL   Top line extends on left

DA   Re-entry (see above)

DB   Re-entry (see above)

DG   Different punch for D used; D enlarged

DI   Different punch for D used; D enlarged

DK   Dot in N.E. corner of K square; D close to right side of square

EG   Dot below G

EH   Fine vertical line in N.E. square close to frame

EK   K close to left side of square

FB   Re-entry (see above)

FF   Several dots in margin below

FH   Blurred dot below and to right of F

FI   Different punch for F used; F enlarged

FK   Dot after K

FL   Scratch through F and ON occurs in late prints only

GF   Dot after top of F

GG   Dot above P and dot in first G

GK   Dot in N.W. corner close to frame

HD   Fresh entry

HF   Right side extends below

HG   Bottom line extends on left

HJ   Left leg of H extends upwards as thick scratch

HK   Left leg of H extends upwards as thick scratch

HL   Small dot close to left side of H square

IH   I well to left side of square

II   I well to right side of square

IK   Top line extends on left

IL   Tiny dot on toe of L

JF   Dot in N.E. square near right side line

JG   Slight burr rub in value; NE joined

JK   Bottom line extends on left

KG   Right foot of K double

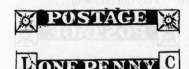

LC   Re-entry (see above)

LG   Top line extends on left

PLATE 55 135

LL One dot before first L; several indistinct dots below same square

OH Short vertical scratch in N.W. corner of H square; horizontal scratch in top of N.W. square

OK Vertical scratch in first N of PENNY in later prints

MB Re-entry (see above)

MH Dot below top right serif of M

PC Re-entry (see above)

MJ Dot after J in late printings

PD Blurred dot in S.E. corner of P square

MK Dot under E of ONE

PF Blurred dot below and to right of P

ML Dot in top of G and dot over L

PG Several dots after G

NJ Dot in toe of E of ONE

PH Blurred dot below and to right of P; top and bottom lines extend on left

PI Blurred dot below and to right of P

NK Dot after N

PL Top line extends on left

NL Large dot in margin above TA

QE Dot after top right serif of E

QG Dot in top of G

QH Right side extends below

OC Re-entry (see above)

QI Dot in front and after I

QJ Right side extends below

RA   Re-entry (see above)

RD   Marked fresh entry

RF   Large dot in top of R

RG   Dot above upright of R

RH   Blur mark in top of R; H high
      and well to right

RI   Dot after I which is very high
      and well to right

RK   Dot below corner of R square

RL   Dot in left fork of Y

SD   Fresh entry, left side strongly
      recut

SF   Mark over F

SG   Mark below N of ONE

SH   Large mark on top of bun; dot
      in S.W. corner of S square

SI   Mark in base of E of PENNY

SJ   Dot in S.E. corner of J square

SL   Top portion of S weak; dot
      above toe of L; two states;
      second state is repair by
      hand retouch

TA   Blurred line lower right corner
      of T and below O

TD   Fresh entry

TE   Fresh entry

TF   Dot in upper part of E of
      POSTAGE

TL   Two states; second state is
      repair by hand retouch;
      large dot below S.E. corner
      of T square

PLATE 56   137

PLATE 56

Summary. Put to press 14.7.1857; withdrawn 2.4.1864; sheets printed not known, but a total of approximately 1,000,000 sheets is likely; Imprimatur sheet in light orange-red on white paper watermarked large crown. There is the slightest trace of blueing in the paper.

Notes. Plate 56 exists only in shades of rose-red on white paper, as printing in the transitional shades ceased just prior to its being put to press.

The plate suffered from the effects of corrosion but not to such a degree as Plate 52. The central part of the plate is the most affected. The N.E. square is strong and the right side generally strong.

The plate was repaired subsequent to printing both by re-entry and hand retouch. NI, OI, QA, TA, TB and TC were affected and exist in two states.

The Watermark is Large Crown and Perforation 14. The plate was used for the temporary perforation 16 issue of December 1857 to March 1858. Mint blocks exist.

The Check Letters are Alphabet III (*g*), except that HA, HB, HC and HD have the tall H of previous plates.

AB   Right side extends below

AE   Dot in base of s and dot in top of E square

BB   Second B has lower serif considerably lengthened

BC   Marks below NE

CA   Right side extends above

CE   Lines of N.E. square cross

CL   Marks within L

DF   Very large dot below PE (see EF)

DG   Fresh entry upper squares, POSTAGE and value

EB   Burr rub TAGE

ED   Lower left serif of E extends to left; mark attached to tip of serif

EF   Dot over ST (see DF)

E·

EL   Dot in front of E

FF   Several marks round second F

FG   Marks in letter squares

FH   Marks around F

GB   Short vertical stroke attached to N.W. corner of G square

GE   Large number of dots in G square

GF   Several marks in F square

GJ   Fresh entry upper squares and POSTAGE

HA   H tall

HB   H tall; several dots in H square

HC   H tall; several dots in H square

HD   H tall, large number of dots in H square and several within D; marks in POSTAGE and on margin above

HE   Large number of dots round H and dot after top corner of E

HF   Large number of dots in both letter squares

HG   Several marks in H square

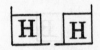

HH   First H high central; second H low central; this stamp is often confused with Reserve Plate 16

HL   Vertical scratch through L

IC   Several dots in C square

PLATE 56 139

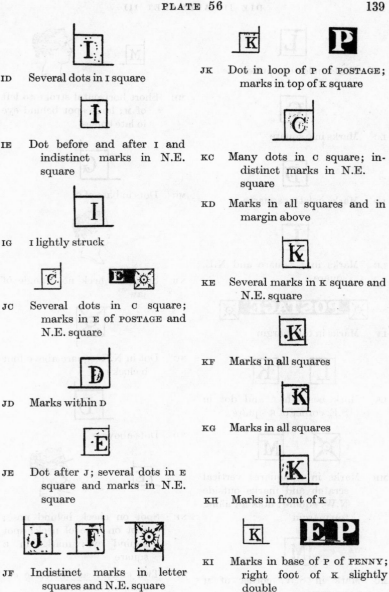

ID   Several dots in I square

IE   Dot before and after I and indistinct marks in N.E. square

IG   I lightly struck

JC   Several dots in C square; marks in E of POSTAGE and N.E. square

JD   Marks within D

JE   Dot after J; several dots in E square and marks in N.E. square

JF   Indistinct marks in letter squares and N.E. square

JI   Ball of J double

JK   Dot in loop of P of POSTAGE; marks in top of K square

KC   Many dots in C square; indistinct marks in N.E. square

KD   Marks in all squares and in margin above

KE   Several marks in K square and N.E. square

KF   Marks in all squares

KG   Marks in all squares

KH   Marks in front of K

KI   Marks in base of P of PENNY; right foot of K slightly double

LA   Marks in A square and N.E. square

LB   Marks in letter squares

LC   Marks in c square

LD   Marks in letter squares

LE   Marks in L square and N.E. square

LF   Marks in top margin

LK   Mark beneath L and dot in S.E. corner of K square

MB   Marks in M square; vertical scratch and marks outside N.W. square; dots all along top margin

MC   Mark in S.W. corner of M square

MD   Marks in M square

ME   Short horizontal stroke to left of M; large spot behind eye in late copies

MG   Dots in base of G

NB   Spot on cheek near angle of jaw

NC   Dot in N.E. square above four o'clock ray

ND   Dots above D

NE   Spot on cheek behind nose; spot on base of neck; spot behind eye; marks in E square

NI   Two states; second state coincident re-entry

OE   Two dots in base of letter O

PLATE **56** 141

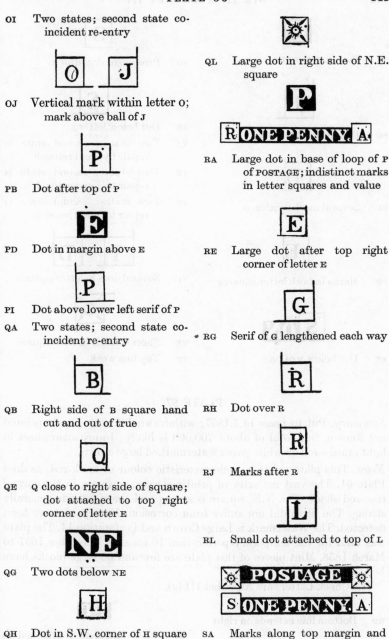

OI Two states; second state co-incident re-entry

OJ Vertical mark within letter O; mark above ball of J

PB Dot after top of P

PD Dot in margin above E

PI Dot above lower left serif of P

QA Two states; second state co-incident re-entry

QB Right side of B square hand cut and out of true

QE Q close to right side of square; dot attached to top right corner of letter E

QG Two dots below NE

QH Dot in S.W. corner of H square and mark after H

QL Large dot in right side of N.E. square

RA Large dot in base of loop of P of POSTAGE; indistinct marks in letter squares and value

RE Large dot after top right corner of letter E

RG Serif of G lengthened each way

RH Dot over R

RJ Marks after R

RL Small dot attached to top of L

SA Marks along top margin and value

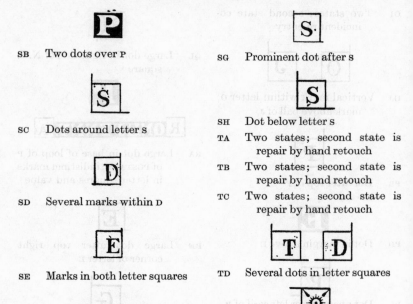

SB Two dots over P	SG Prominent dot after s
SC Dots around letter s	SH Dot below letter s
	TA Two states; second state is repair by hand retouch
SD Several marks within D	TB Two states; second state is repair by hand retouch
	TC Two states; second state is repair by hand retouch
SE Marks in both letter squares	TD Several dots in letter squares
	TE Short scratch in N.E. square
SF Dot below N of ONE	TH Top line weak

PLATE 57

Summary. Put to press 14.7.1857; withdrawn 1.3.1864; sheets printed not known, but total of about 700,000 is likely; Imprimatur sheet in light orange-red on white paper watermarked large crown.

Notes. This plate exists in a characteristic colour of brick-red, as does Plate 61. The vast majority of printings were, however, in the normal rose-red shade. The N.E. square is strong and the right side generally strong. The plate did not suffer from corrosion. No repairs have been detected. The Watermark is Large Crown and Perforation 14. The plate was used for the temporary perforation 16 issue of December 1857 to March 1858. Mint pieces of this plate are few and no large blocks have been seen.

The Check Letters are Alphabet III (*g*).

BB Bottom line extends on right	
	BI Large dot over P attached to top line; line on top loop of B
BF Right side extends below	

PLATE 57   143

BJ   Fresh entry upper square; tiny dot in upper part of O of ONE and in right L and fork of Y

HJ   Fresh entry upper squares and in margin above

HK   H double above

BL   Several dots in front of B

CF   Dot in margin opposite back of neck

HL   H slightly taller than normal; different punch used; scratch in N.W. corner of H square

DA   Blurred mark below S.W. corner of A square

IE   Bottom line extends slightly on right

IK   Bottom line extends on left

JE   Bottom line extends on right

DD   Dot in P of POSTAGE on all except early printings

ED   Blurred mark within D in early printings

JL   Dot in lower portion of N.E. square

KC   Top and bottom lines extend slightly on right

KF   Dot below S.W. corner of K square

EH   Evidence of double H on left

FE   Different punch for F used; F tall

GA   Top line extends slightly on right

KL   Top margin weak

ML   M double at top on left

HF   F well to right side of square

HG   Dot in letter G

HH   Dot below S.E. corner of second H square

NK   Tiny dot under left foot of N

OB   Dot below S.E. corner of B square

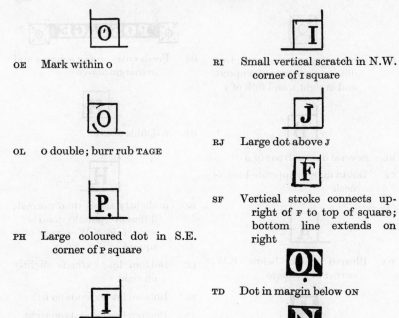

OE   Mark within o

OL   o double; burr rub TAGE

PH   Large coloured dot in S.E.
corner of P square

PI   I slightly double below

RC   Top line extends on left

RI   Small vertical scratch in N.W.
corner of I square

RJ   Large dot above J

SF   Vertical stroke connects upright of F to top of square;
bottom line extends on
right

TD   Dot in margin below ON

TE   Scratch into margin from left
foot of second N

PLATE 58

Summary. Put to press 14.7.1857; defaced 29.10.1861; sheets printed 408,000; Imprimatur sheet in light orange-red on white paper water-marked large crown.

Notes. This plate suffered badly from the effects of corrosion which is spread over its entirety. The N.E. square is weak, very markedly so in the late printings, and the right side has the usual weakness. This indicates that it was laid down by a different roller to that used for Plates 52–57. The Queen's head is generally weak so that 'cameo heads' are very frequent.

The Watermark is Large Crown and Perforation 14. The plate was used for the temporary perforation 16 issue of December 1857 to March 1858.

The colour varies from a deep rose-red to a normal rose-red, later printings being slightly paler in colour.

TD and TI were repaired by re-entry and exist in two states. Mint pieces of this plate are few and no large blocks have been seen.

The Check Letters are Alphabet III (*g*).

PLATE 58   145

AE   Dot before E

AI   Large spot in margin above I square; two dots below N of ONE

AK   Dot on margin above N.E. square

BD   Dot in left leg of A

BF   Dot in base of T

BH   Large irregular mark on back of neck; left lower serif of H extends and nearly touches left side of square; large dot in top of G

CB   Several marks on shoulder

CD   Mark in D and after it; probably remains of original entry of O in error

K

CE   Dot in nose and in base of P of POSTAGE

CJ   Dot in lower part of C

CK   Dot to left of upper left serif of K; dot in back of G

DG   Spot on nose

DH   Large number of small spots on nose and mouth

DJ   Right side extends below

DK   Several marks in base of N.E. square

EB   Dot in N.E. corner of E square

EG   Two dots in second N of PENNY

EH   Dot below ear

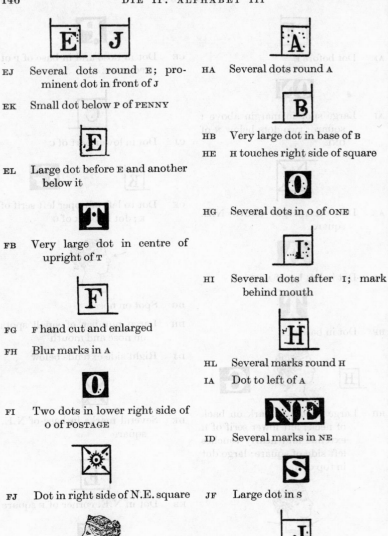

EJ　Several dots round E; prominent dot in front of J

EK　Small dot below P of PENNY

EL　Large dot before E and another below it

FB　Very large dot in centre of upright of T

FG　F hand cut and enlarged

FH　Blur marks in A

FI　Two dots in lower right side of O of POSTAGE

FJ　Dot in right side of N.E. square

GB　Several spots on nostril

GL　Dot in base of G

HA　Several dots round A

HB　Very large dot in base of B

HE　H touches right side of square

HG　Several dots in O of ONE

HI　Several dots after I; mark behind mouth

HL　Several marks round H

IA　Dot to left of A

ID　Several marks in NE

JF　Large dot in S

JK　Two small marks after J

JL　Small dot on tip of nose

PLATE 58   147

KD   Spot over eye; dots on cheek and chin

KL   Right foot of K double

LA   Large number of dots in value and A square

LD   Several dots round L

LF   Marks in EN and several marks round F

LG   G double and marks after G; large dot in base of P and E and base of second N of PENNY

LH   Large dot over L; many marks in H square; many dots in bottom margin

LI   Many dots in L square; large dots in base of E PEN

LJ   Many dots in L square and O of ONE; dot before J and outside right side of J square

LK   Dots in L and K squares; large dot in base of EN; dots below base of stamp

LL   Dot and stroke before second L

MA   Dot in back of G

MG   Spot on cheek behind mouth; dot in right side of O of POSTAGE

MH   Several dots in N.E. square

MI   Mark in base of N.W. square; dot in right hand side of N.E. square

MJ   Several dots in J square; mark on right side below N.E. square

MK   Dots in M and K squares and P of POSTAGE

ML   Dot in top of G; mark in base of P of POSTAGE

NC   Bottom line extends on right

ND   Several dots in O of POSTAGE

NG   G hand cut and enlarged; several dots in S.E. corner of G square; different roller used for laying down impression; N.E. square strong; head stronger than normal for this plate; possibly a coincident re-entry with letters hand cut subsequently

NH   Marks above s; N hand cut and slightly enlarged

NK   Large dot in toe of E of POST-AGE; dot over N.E. square; two dots in front of K; marks around N

NL   Vertical scratch outside upper half of right side; dot in left side of letter N; many dots on top margin

OB   Dots in O; dots after B

     E

OC   Dots in letter O and E of ONE

OD   Dots in letter squares and in top of O of ONE

OE   Mark after O and in base of ONE

OF   Dot above F

OG   Dots in O square

OH   Several dots round H; dot in top of P of PENNY

OI   Dot in toe of E of ONE and P of PENNY; several dots round I

OJ   Dot to left of O and several dots within curve of J

OK   Many dots in O; large dot in toe of E and base of P of POSTAGE

Q–B (Top)

PB   Many horizontal scratches in lower part of value and in lower margin; many dots in B square

PC   Many dots in P square; large dot in base of P of PENNY; dots below E P

PD   Many dots around P

NN

PE   Several spots in NN and in margin beneath NN

PF   Two marks before P

PG   Large dot attached to top of P also blurred mark; dot in base of P of PENNY

H

PH   Horizontal scratches and tiny dots in bottom margin; H close to right; top right serif cuts through side of square

PI   Dot after I

PLATE 58   149

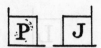

PJ   Several dots round P; bottom line extends on right

PK   Dot attached to top of P

PL   Large dot before base of P

QB   Many tiny dots in POSTAGE and in margin above

QC   Many tiny dots in POSTAGE and in margin above, generally faint

QD   Many tiny dots in POSTAGE upper squares and in margin above

QE   Many tiny dots in N.W. square and G

QF   Large spot on cheek on early prints; dots in Q and N.W. square

QG   Both letters hand cut and enlarged; different roller used; N.E. square strong and head stronger than usual; right side strong; possibly coincident re-entry with letters hand cut subsequently; dot in upper part of S

QI   Large dot in Q

QL   Two dots in front of Q

RA   Large dot in base of E of PENNY; A touches right side of square

RB   Dot attached to upper loop of B

RD   Two dots in front of R

RE   Dot over R and in front of E

RF   Mark in front of R

RG   Both letters hand cut and enlarged; different roller used; N.E. square strong and head stronger than usual; right side strong; possibly coincident re-entry with letters hand cut subsequently; horizontal scratch connects left foot of R to left side of square

RH   Dot in front of R

RI   Dot in left side of N.E. square

RK   Two dots in R square and several dots in E PE

RL   Large dot after R

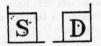

SB   Large dot below P

SD   Several dots in S square; dot in D

SE   Several dots in S square; large dots in E PE and below second N

SF   Dot in right side of N.W. square

SK   Mark in right side of N.W. square; horizontal scratch connects lower left serif of K to left side of square and continues into full stop

SL   Dot outside S.E. corner of L square

TC   Dot in base of P of POSTAGE

TD   Two states; second state coincident re-entry; dots in N.E. square in early first state

TE   Marks in N.W. square

TI   Two states; second state coincident re-entry; dot in toe of E of POSTAGE persists

TJ   Several dots round T; dot after J

TK   Dot over T and large dot in top of G

PLATE 59

Summary. Put to press 14.7.1857; withdrawn 2.4.1864; sheets printed 805,200; Imprimatur sheet in dull orange-rose on white paper, which shows a trace of blueing, watermarked large crown.

Notes. Corrosion did not affect this plate. The N.E. square is weak and right side has the usual weakness in the lower third. The N.E. square is not as weak as that of Plate 58; a different roller therefore had been used. The N.W. square is slightly weak on this plate.

The colour varies from a deep rose-red to a normal rose-red, later printings being slightly paler in colour.

PLATE **59** 151

The Watermark is Large Crown and Perforation 14. The plate was used for the temporary perforation 16 issue of December 1857 to March 1858.

No repairs have been noted. Large mint blocks are known and the plate exists in mint state complete.

The Check Letters are Alphabet III (*g*).

AG Scratch across point of chin in late printings

AI Mark in front of top of A

AK Mark in toe of E of ONE

BB Small mark over top of second B

BE Blur over full stop

BF Blurred mark below and to left of lower left serif of F

BH Mark below left foot of H

BI Scratch from corner of eye to lobe of ear in late printings; dot on top of B

BJ Dots on bust

BK B with lower serif lengthened

BL Vertical scratch outside N.W. square

CI Re-entry upper squares, POST-AGE and value

CJ Dot attached to base of curve of J

CK Dot in middle bar of E of POSTAGE

CL Dot in middle of S

DH Right side extends slightly below

DI Blurred dot in right side of A in late printings

DJ Scratch across shoulder in intermediate printings; disappears in later printings

DK Base line weak, NE joined in late printings

DL Upper serif of D lengthened

EC Dot in base of upright of E of POSTAGE

EE   Top and bottom lines extend on right

EG   Marks in margin well below NN (see FG)

EH   E close to right side of square

EJ   Top line extends on right; E nearly touches right side of square

EK   Left foot of K double

FD   Dot near corner of N.W. square

FG   Marks on margin above G (see EG)

FJ   Scratch extends from shoulder through E of ONE into margin in intermediate printings

GG   Dot in right segment of N.E. square and dot on cheek

GK   Large spot of tip on nose

HB   Small dot above right upright of H

HC   Upper portion of C slightly double

HI   In intermediate printings, vertical scratch runs from right fork of Y into margin to reach II; disappears in late printings

HJ   Large dot attached to centre of top line of N.E. square

IB   Top line extends on right

ID   I very close to right

IE   Top line extends on right

IF   Scratch extends from upper left major ray in N.E. square into margin above in same straight line; nearly reaches the Y of HF

JH   Bottom line extends on right

JJ   Large dot attached to left side of second J square

KL   Horizontal scratch in N.E. square

LJ   Dot in left side of O of POSTAGE, except in early printings

ML   M very high central

NB   N hand cut and enlarged; left upright extends slightly below serif

PLATE 59   153

NF   Vertical scratch in N.W. square well wide of frame

NH   Right upright of N is prolonged slightly downwards

OB   Dot above lower serif of B

OI   Top right serif of I extends to right

PG   Slight indentation into base of O of ONE

QG   Re-entry upper square

RD   Different roller used; N.E. square and right side firm; right side extends below

RF   Blur within top of R

RG   Marks of former entry of QG along top margin and N.W. square

RJ   Dot in loop of R; large spot between J square and R square of RK

RK   Dot in base of E of PENNY; large spot between R square and J square of RJ

RL   Large dot within L

SC   Upper portion of C slightly double

SF   Right side extends below

SH   S close to left side of square

SK   Lower right serif of K slightly double

SL   Scratch in margin parallel with right side

TE   Tiny dot close to top right corner of E

TF   Re-entry upper squares, POSTAGE, value and F square; spot on tip of nose

TH   Marked burr rub TAGE and N.E. square

TI   Small mark in upper right fork of Y

TJ   Large dot in right segment of N.E. square

TK   Dot below second N of PENNY;
      dot in foot of E of POSTAGE

TL   Dot below NY

PLATE 60

Summary. Put to press 14.7.1857; withdrawn 1.3.1864; sheets printed not known, but a total of nearly 1,000,000 is likely; Imprimatur sheet in bright orange-red on white paper, which shows a very slight trace of blueing, watermarked large crown.

Notes. The N.E. square is very weak on this plate and the right side has the usual weakness in the lower third; it is weaker than on plate 59. The check letters are unusually bold, somewhat thicker than usual and many stamps may be picked out by this means. The colour is often a deep rose-red, becoming less intense as the plate became worn.

The Watermark is Large Crown and Perforation 14. This is the last plate that was used for the temporary perforation 16 issue of December 1857 to March 1858.

No repairs have been noted. A few mint pieces are known.

The Check Letters are Alphabet III (*g*).

AD   Mark in N.W. square occurs on all copies except the very earliest printings; D is very high to right

CD   Dot in upper part of D except in early printings

CG   Faint stroke in upper portion of G

AK   Dots in N.W. square and on margin above

DB   Faint horizontal scratch through top of head

DD   Top line extends on right

BI   Marked re-entry upper squares, POSTAGE and value

DE   Dash attached to upper right corner of E

PLATE 60   155

EB	B hand cut and much enlarged
EJ	Right side extends above

FB	Marked re-entry upper squares, POSTAGE and value

FC	Upper portion of C double

FD	Vertical stroke in front of F

FL	Upper left serif of F extended to left

GC	Upper portion of C double

HC	H very close to right side of square; dot in C

HF	Lower right serif extends to touch side of square

HL	H double below

IB	Mark in upright of P of POSTAGE

JF	Mark in upper left portion of E of POSTAGE

KJ	Blurred marks on K

ME	Dash attached to upper right serif of E

NC	Marks in margin below from original entry of OC; dot below E of ONE
ND	Middle bar of N slightly prolonged downwards

OC	Re-entry upper squares, POSTAGE and on margin above

OF	Several dots in O which is close to right side of square; only the upper dot persists
QB	Top line extends on right

QC	C hand cut, enlarged and rounded
QL	Bottom line extends on right

RE   Dot in top of R

RH   Blur in lower part of H

SG   Blur on lower part of s

SL   Blur on letter s except in late printings

TA   Scratch through base of Y extends into A square except in early printings

TI   Bottom line extends on right

TK   Top right ray in N.E. square hand cut, thickened and out of position

PLATE 61

Summary. Put to press 8.5.1858; taken from press 30.5.1861; defaced 29.10.1861; sheets printed 186,100; Imprimatur sheet in rose-red on white paper watermarked large crown.

Notes. The N.E. square is strong and right side firm. This printing nearly always occurs in a shade of brick-red and may be recognised by this means after study. The Watermark is Large Crown and Perforation 14.

Repair by re-entry was carried out on CL, DL, EL, FL and GL subsequent to the plate being at press, and it thus exists in two states. HL, IL, JL, KL, LL, ML and NL were all re-entered prior to the plate going to press.

Only one large mint piece has been seen, together with a few small pieces.

The Check Letters are Alphabet III (*g*).

BA   Bottom line extends on right

CL   Two states; second state coincident re-entry

DL   Two states; second state coincident re-entry

EG   G to right and high

EL   Two states; second state coincident re-entry

FB   Right side extends slightly below

FL   Two states; second state coincident re-entry

GL   Two states; second state coincident re-entry

HE   H to right

HL   Coincident re-entry

IL   Coincident re-entry; dot in base of loop of P of POSTAGE

JK   Spot on nose

PLATE 61 157

JL   Coincident re-entry

KL   Coincident re-entry; large spot attached to right side of L square

LF   Marks above and to right of F

LG   G double

LH   Numerous marks in H square

LI   Dot to right of foot of L; re-entry in value

LL   Mark to left of foot of L

MG   Bottom line extends slightly on left; dot in O of POSTAGE

MH   Right side extends slightly below; marks in N.W. and S.E. corners of N.E. square

MJ   Mark in centre of right frame line

MK   Marks in P of POSTAGE

ML   Coincident re-entry

ND   Dot below S.E. corner of D square

NG   Blur to right of foot of G

NH   Diagonal of N extended

NK   N leaning forward: line above top right serif

OD   Mark to right centre of O

OE   O to right and joined to frame by blob; lines under N and E of ONE

OF   Tiny dot in S.W. corner of F square

OI   Vertical scratch in letter O

OJ   J blurred

OK   Dots in O and in right of O square

PC   Top line extends slightly on right

PD   Two dots to right of loop of P

PE   Blurred dot near S.E. corner of P square

PF   Mark to left centre of P and below

PH   Foot of P double

PI   Dot to right centre of I

PK   Dot above loop of P to right

PL   Dot to left of foot of P

QG   Q to left; dot below left side of Q square

RE   Linear blur across S.W. corner of R square

RI   Dot inside loop of R

RK   Marks in margin below from SK fresh entry; dot to right of R

RL   Dot to right of R

SA   Blur attached to left side of A square

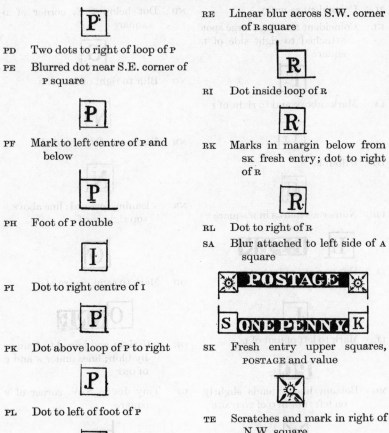

SK   Fresh entry upper squares, POSTAGE and value

TE   Scratches and mark in right of N.W. square

TJ   Dots above and across T

PLATE 62

Summary. Put to press 5.12.1859; withdrawn 1.3.1864; sheets printed not known, but 375,000 would be likely; Imprimatur sheet in rose-red on white paper watermarked large crown.

Notes. The N.E. square is strong and right side firm. The printings are in a moderately constant shade of rose-red throughout. The Watermark is Large Crown, Perforation 14. The plate has several fine examples of misplaced entries, all of which were corrected, and the traces of the former entries show up well.

PLATE 62   159

No repairs have been noted. Large mint blocks exist and the plate is shown in mint condition complete.

The Check Letters are Alphabet III (*g*).

AE Marks in value and letter squares and margin below from original entry of BE; E hand cut and enlarged

AK Large dot in S.E. corner of A square

AL L high central

BC Dot within lower part of C

BE Marks of re-entry upper squares

BF Marks above F

BH Mark over and after B

BL Top line weak over TAGE

DI Dot above lower right serif of I

DJ Scratch across back of neck on intermediate printings

EH Diagonal scratch runs from second square jewel through ear to shoulder in intermediate printings

EI Scratch in left side of N.E. square extends into margin

FD Dot in front of top of D

FI Dot close to right side two-thirds way down

GG Vertical scratch runs from front jewel through back of eye downwards through tip of bust and on through lower left serif of E of ONE, through margin into top of O of POSTAGE of HG; this occurs in intermediate printings

GH   Vertical scratch joins o of ONE to P of POSTAGE on HH in intermediate printings; vertical scratch in left side of N.W. square and G square

GI   G hand cut and slightly enlarged

GK   Dot in top of K

GL   Dot on middle of neck

HJ   Scratch runs from corner of eye, parallel to and near front line of neck to edge of shoulder; vertical scratch in right side of H square

HK   Dot in lower loop of P of POSTAGE and mark in base of same P

IF   Vertical scratch runs through F square in intermediate printings

IH   Scratch behind upper right serif of I

KH   Scratch on back of neck in intermediate printings; thick scratch in S.E. corner of K square proceeds down towards LH

KJ   J hand cut and slightly enlarged

LH   Thick scratch from KH runs in top margin down into top of P of POSTAGE; serif forming toe of L almost absent

LK   Re-entry upper squares, POSTAGE and value

MB   Right side extends below

MF   Horizontal scratch in top of F square

MG   Scratch on back of letter G

MK   Circular blur mark on margin over PO

PLATE 62   161

ND   Vertical mark in top of D

NF   Dot below foot of letter N

NG   Dot below foot of letter N

NH   H struck slightly too softly

NI   N hand cut and slightly en-
      larged; dot after I near top;
      scratch connects top right
      serif of N to side of square in
      early printings

NJ   Both letters hand cut and
      slightly enlarged; small
      mark after J

NL   Top margin weak

OB   Top line extends on right

PA   Bottom line extends on right

PF   Upper left serif of P extends
      backwards

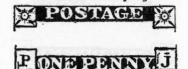

PJ   Strong re-entry all squares,
      POSTAGE, value and top and
      bottom margins; J hand cut
      and lower loop flattened

L

PL   Bottom line extends on left

QD   Large dot in right side of O of
      POSTAGE

QI   Horizontal mark in upper part
      of N.E. square

QJ   Marked re-entry all squares,
      POSTAGE, value and on top
      and bottom margins; J hand
      cut and lower loop slightly
      flattened

RC   Re-entry letter squares and
      value

RD   R very high

RF   Tiny dot attached to base of
      upright of R

RG   Back of G double near top;
      only visible on early print-
      ings

RH   Blurred mark attached to loop
      of R

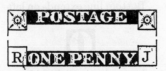

RJ   Marked re-entry all squares, POSTAGE, value, top and bottom margins; J hand cut and lower loop slightly flattened

SF   Marked re-entry all squares, POSTAGE, value and on bottom margin; both letters hand cut

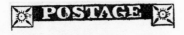

SJ   Marked re-entry all squares, POSTAGE, value and on bottom margin; both letters hand cut

SK   Burr rub in value

SL   Very marked re-entry all squares, POSTAGE, value and on top and bottom margins; both letters hand cut

TC   C close to right side of square
TF   Top right serif of T very weak

TH   Dot in central part of S

TI   Dot in top of E of POSTAGE; vertical scratch in right side of I square; vertical scratch on cheek

TJ   Marked re-entry all squares, POSTAGE, value and on bottom margin; both letters hand cut

TK   Re-entry upper squares, POSTAGE, and value

TL   Very marked re-entry all squares, POSTAGE, value and on top and bottom margins; both letters hand cut and slightly enlarged

PLATE 63   163

PLATE 63

Summary. Put to press 5.3.1860; taken from press 30.5.1861; defaced 29.10.1861; sheets printed 145,100; Imprimatur sheet in rose-red on white paper watermarked large crown.

Notes. The N.E. square is strong and the right side firm. The engraving generally is weak, particularly of the Queen's head which has the 'cameo appearance' frequently; this may be the reason for the plate's short life. No repairs have been noted. The plate is scarce in mint condition and only a few blocks have been seen.

The Check Letters are Alphabet III (*g*).

		LA	Dot above toe of L; right side extends below
BI	Tiny dot between B and N.E. corner of square	LE	Dot above upright of E; vertical scratch down right margin; top line extends on right
		ME	Top line extends slightly on right
		OJ	Top line extends on right
GE	Large dot on margin between E and N.W. corner of N.E. square	PA	Cross bar of A faint; its lower right serif extends to right
		QF	Right side extends below
GF	Top line weak	QJ	Bottom line extends on right
IE	Dot below S.E. corner of E square	RK	Dot after top right serif of K
JF	Bottom line extends on left		
KI	Left side extends below		
KK	Right side of N.E. square thickened	SK	Dot attached to foot of upright of K
KL	Top line extends on right	TK	Foot of K slightly double

PLATE 64

Summary. Put to press 5.11.1860; defaced 29.10.1861; sheets printed 19,400; Imprimatur sheet in rose-red on white paper watermarked large crown.

Notes. The N.E. square is strong and the right side firm. The printings are very rare and few examples of this plate have been seen even in used condition. It contains two of the most marked misplaced entries in this Die 2 group. TB and TL show most pronounced marks of the former entries; they are the most eagerly looked for fresh entries. TC and TD were re-entered before issue but this was coincident in both cases.

The Check Letters are Alphabet III (g).

CH Lower right serif of H extends to right side of square

EA Small mark in top left portion of O of POSTAGE

EE Bottom line extends slightly on right

EH Short vertical scratch in N.E corner of H square

EI Scratch runs from top right serif of E into O of ONE, becoming thicker during its course from E to O

FK Lower right serif of K double

LF Blur attached to back of L

MH Lower right serif of H extends to margin

OJ Left and right sides extend slightly above

QA Blurred mark in right side of O of ONE

QF Bottom line extends on left

RD Strong blur in horizontal bar of second N of PENNY

RG Right side extends below

RH Right side extends slightly below

TB Marked re-entry all squares, POSTAGE and value

TC Marked re-entry; left side double; base of T square noticeably double

TD Coincident re-entry; burr line runs down both margins; T and D slightly thinned

TJ Tiny dot above corner of N.E. square

TL Very strong re-entry all squares, POSTAGE, value, top and bottom margins

PLATE 65

Summary. Put to press 14.1.1861; defaced 29.10.1861; sheets printed 10,600; Imprimatur sheet in rose-red on white paper watermarked large crown.

Notes. The N.E. square is strong and the right side firm. The printings are extremely rare and very few specimens of this plate have been seen. The reason for this is that the plate was condemned at first as being too irregularly laid down for perforation. Subsequently it is thought that the 10,600 sheets printed were sufficiently well perforated to be issued.*

There are two misplaced entries RL and TL; these are of the utmost rarity. Both are well marked.

The Check Letters are Alphabet III (g).

* See *The Line Engraved Postage Stamps of Great Britain*, by Sir E. D. Bacon, pp. 160–161.

PLATE 65   165

DE   Dot outside N.E. corner of
      N.E. square

PA   Slight burr rub in value,
      especially in E of PENNY

PH   Top line weak

QE   Small blur to top of right of E

RL   Marked re-entry all squares,
      POSTAGE, and value; both
      letters hand cut and en-
      larged

TJ   Top line very weak

TL   Marked re-entry in N.W.
      square, value and on margin
      below

PLATE 66

Summary. Put to press 13.2.1861; withdrawn 17.3.1864; sheets printed not known, but estimated at 325,000; Imprimatur sheet in rose-red on white paper watermarked large crown, which is inverted.

Notes. The N.E. square is strong and the right side firm.

This plate was used for the 'Royal reprint', which was done in black.*

The printings are all in pale rose and pale pink. True rose-red does not exist. The Perforation is 14 and Watermarked Large Crown.

Mint blocks exist. No repair has been noted.

The Check Letters are Alphabet III (*g*).

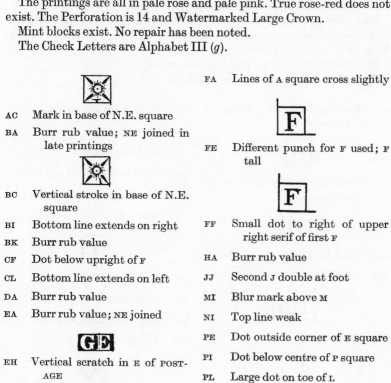

AC   Mark in base of N.E. square

BA   Burr rub value; NE joined in
      late printings

BC   Vertical stroke in base of N.E.
      square

BI   Bottom line extends on right

BK   Burr rub value

CF   Dot below upright of F

CL   Bottom line extends on left

DA   Burr rub value

EA   Burr rub value; NE joined

EH   Vertical scratch in E of POST-
      AGE

FA   Lines of A square cross slightly

FE   Different punch for F used; F
      tall

FF   Small dot to right of upper
      right serif of first F

HA   Burr rub value

JJ   Second J double at foot

MI   Blur mark above M

NI   Top line weak

PE   Dot outside corner of E square

PI   Dot below centre of P square

PL   Large dot on toe of L

* *The Line Engraved Postage Stamps of Great Britain,* by Sir E. D. Bacon, pp. 167–168.

QE	Blur attached to right side of Q square
RA	Burr rub value

SA	Burr rub value; marks in right side of A square
SE	Dot near N.W. corner of N.W. square
SL	Blur after top of L
TE	Bottom line extends slightly on left

RF   Blur in right side of R square

PLATE 67

Summary. Put to press 13.2.1862; withdrawn 1.3.1864; sheets printed 250,400; Imprimatur sheet in rose-red on white paper watermarked large crown.

Notes. The N.E. square is strong and right side firm.

The printings are all in a pale rose-pink, which was deeper with the first sheets; true rose-red does not exist. The Perforation is 14 and Watermarked Large Crown.

Mint blocks exist. No repair has been noted.

The Check Letters are Alphabet III (*g*).

AL	Horizontal line close to base of L square

FB	Mark in left side of O of ONE
FK	Burr rub value
GA	Burr rub value
GB	Mark in left side of O of ONE
GC	Blur in upper part of letter G
GK	Burr rub value

BF	Mark attached to base of B
CK	Burr rub value

DB	Mark in left side of O of ONE
DK	Burr rub value

IH	Dot attached to top of I
JA	Burr rub value; NE joined
LA	Burr rub value; NE joined
LE	Dot above toe of L

EB	Mark in left side of O of ONE

EL	L very high and close to left side of square

MB   Large spot on neck

PLATE 67   167

oc	Large spot on cheek
ra	Burr rub value
rg	Large dot in top of r
rh	Dot in top of r
rk	Tiny dot after lower right serif of k
sa	Burr rub value; ne joined

sl	Tiny dot near upper right corner of s square
ta	Mark in right side of o of one
th	t very high central

PLATE 68

Summary. Put to press 9.1.1862; withdrawn 1.3.1864; sheets printed not known, but estimated at 150,000; Imprimatur sheet in rose-red on white paper watermarked large crown.

Notes. The N.E. square is strong and right side firm. The engravings on the entire plate are weak so that 'cameo heads' are very frequent.

The colour is nearly characteristic of the plate. It is a pale rust colour but printings occur in the usual rose-pink of the period, particularly those at the beginning of the plate's life.

The Perforation is 14 and Watermarked Large Crown.

Mint pieces are few. No repair has been noted.

The Check Letters are Alphabet III (*g*).

ag	Re-entry upper squares, post-age and value
ba	Right side extends above
bg	Top line weak

bi	Large spot near base of neck

fa	a very high to right
gc	Vertical scratch in upper part of c

ie	Burr rub value; fresh entry marks in margin below from je

LG   G double

IF   Fresh entry marks in margin below from JF

LK   Bottom line extends on left; top line extends on right

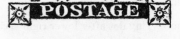

JE   Well marked fresh entry all squares, POSTAGE and value

NC   Fresh entry; well marked

JF   Well marked fresh entry all squares and POSTAGE

PH   Large spot on face below eye; several spots on tip of bust

JG   J high central

KA   Horizontal scratch across A square

KE   Bottom line extends very slightly on right

PI   Several small spots on cheek

KK   Large dot after middle of second K

QE   Bottom line extends on left; several marks on bust

QG   Bottom line extends slightly on left

RA   Right side extends below

RL   Top line weak

KL   Fresh entry upper squares, POSTAGE and on margin above, and value

SD   Base line weak; lower serif of D prolonged

PLATE 68   169

SE   Base line weak

SG   Burr rub value; NE joined

TF   Mark attached to lower right
      serif of T

TI   Dot very close to top of up-
      right of T

RESERVE PLATE 17

Summary. Put to press April 1862; withdrawn 1.3.1864; sheets printed 191,200; Imprimatur sheet in a plum shade on blue paper watermarked small crown.

Notes. The shade of rose-red at this period was a pinkish colour, so that printings in true rose-red do not exist. The colour remained fairly uniform until the plate was withdrawn.

The plate was completed in June 1855 and held in reserve until needed. During its period of non-use it became slightly affected by corrosion. This chiefly attacked the letter squares, causing blurring. It became less noticeable as the plate grew older. There is no evidence that it was ever withdrawn for cleaning.

The main interest in this plate lies in its characteristic letters. It should be placed in a sub-group of Alphabet III on its own. It is possible to describe only certain of them.

The letter K is semi-Gothic, the lower horizontal bar being placed slightly high so as to join the upper distal to the upright; the letter S is abnormally tall; the letter H is squat, rather broad, and somewhat larger than the letter H of sub-group (*g*).

The letter L is tall, thin, and has a broken back appearance, the lower bar falling downwards to form an obtuse angle; the letter E is small, thin, has a broken back appearance with pronounced serifs, and the middle bar is placed too high.

The letter M is broad, resembling the M of sub-groups (*a*) and (*b*), but the up strokes are very thin and the down strokes very thick. It is smaller than the early type of M.

The letter B has the top and bottom loops the same size, with the top and bottom of the letter weak; the letter P has a wide loop, but this is somewhat smaller than the P of sub-groups (*a*), (*b*) and (*c*).

After long study it is possible to separate all 240 stamps, for all the letters differ very slightly from their counterparts. This was effected for the first time during 1946, when Dr Wiggins and Mr H. F. Johnson produced a photographic reproduction of the reconstruction.

MA (ML)   TA (TL)

Errors of the Large Crown watermarks

The Watermark is Large Crown and the Perforation 14. The error of watermark is known (MA); also the inverted watermark.

Up to date the stamp has not been seen used abroad.

There are two fresh entries:

RI. This shows principally in the N.W. square and slightly in the N.E. square. The left side of the stamp is heavily blurred, as in SI, and

there are marks above SI, the original entry of RI being placed one-eighth of an inch too low. A mint block shows ONE PE very clearly in the gutter margin between RI and SI.

JF. This shows in the upper squares and POSTAGE.

There are the following varieties:

BE   Dot in lower part of O of ONE

DJ   Ball of foot of J double

GD   Large spot on face

OD   D close to right and tilted

OE   o doubled

OG   o doubled; mark in o at bottom

RL   R to right and low

TC   T to right

TF   Vertical mark attached to the lower frame line of T square below and to left of the T

The letters L in the vertical L row are nearly all placed too high.

Only two large mint blocks are known; one of the upper five rows and another of twenty-five from part of the lower three rows with side margins, inscription and Plate R17.

Chapter Five

Fourth Issue of One Penny Perforated

PLATES 50 and 51

DIE II: ALPHABET IV

This alphabet was an experiment, made in the middle of 1856, and the check letters, instead of being punched in, were engraved by hand on these two plates. The result was considered unsatisfactory, and the older method was reverted to from Plate 52 onwards.

These distinctive letters were recognized at the beginning of the study of the red One Penny stamps, but it was not until Sir E. D. Bacon discovered the entry in the Perkins, Bacon engraving book that it was realized that they were hand engraved.

These plates were held in reserve and were put to press in 1861, after the construction of the One Penny plates from the original Die I had been discontinued. This explains the fact that while the imprimatur sheets of both plates were registered in red-brown on blued paper the issued stamps appeared in rose-red on white paper. The plates were completed on 11th June 1856. Plate 50 was registered on 27th June and Plate 51 one day earlier.

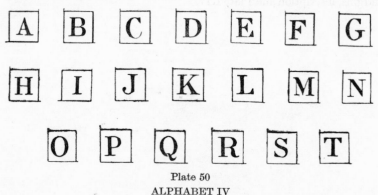

Plate 50
ALPHABET IV

As will be seen from the illustrations of the characteristics of the Alphabet IV check letters, they are generally very much larger than those of Alphabets I to III.

Faint, but well-defined, dots are found close to the check letters on

172

Plate 50, and are clearly visible on the imprimatur examples. II and TC have dots on both sides of the lower serifs, which were evidently intentional. Visible examples on the issued stamps are illustrated.

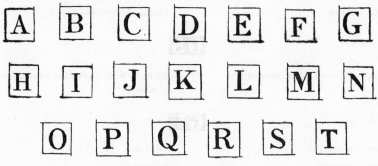

Plate 51
ALPHABET IV

Plate 51 was retouched before it was put to press. This is clearly shown by a study of the imprimatur examples. The side lines have been re-cut almost throughout and the N.E. square attended to in many places. Dr H. Osborne, in his book *Repaired Impressions*, has published an exhaustive survey of the nature of this repair, in which it is proved that several stamps appear in two states, and more recently he and Dr Wiggins have demonstrated that two copies of KB with the re-cut N.E. square occur in a third state.†

While at press Plate 51 appears to have sustained some damage, as later printings show marks and blotches which do not appear on earlier printings, such as CJ, which shows a diagonal scratch on the face, and CK a cut on the forehead.

Both plates, however, are unusually free from errors, flaws and accidental marks, of which the more defined are given for plating purposes, and those illustrated are marked with an asterisk (*).

PLATE 50	PLATE 51

| AA | Both letters high | Burr right of first A* |

| AE | Foot of E extended* | E slightly larger |

† *The Stamp Lover*, Vol. XLIII, March–April 1951, p. 166.

	PLATE 50	PLATE 51

AJ	A low	Dot under second N of PENNY*

BA	Burr on right margin	Blur in S of POSTAGE, sometimes absent*

BB	B central	Blur in E of POSTAGE*
BC	C round	C narrow
BE	E central	E high to left

BJ	Small dot left of J*	Both letters to left

BL	Mark right of L*	B to left
CB	B central	B far to left

CD	Small dot right of C*	D much smaller

CI	C central	C to left, spot touches outer curve, but not constant*

DE	Oblique mark on top margin*	E to left
DG	G very large	G much smaller, to left
DI	I central	I to left

PLATE 50	PLATE 51
EB E broad, B smaller	E narrow, B broader
EF E large, low	F small, high left
FC F narrow, slightly left	F wider, more to left

FD Faint mark close to D*	D to left

GB Both letters larger, and more central	Blur in N.E. square; letters to left*

GE Large G, E more central	Small oblique mark in N.W. square, E left*

HA Dots both sides at top of A*	H slightly higher

HF Small dot in F*	F taller, to left
IB Letters more central	B far to left

IJ J more to left	Diagonal scratch right of I*

JA Small dot after J*	J more to left

JD D smaller	J central. Stop after PENNY cuts into corner square*

PLATE 50   **PLATE 51**

JL   Lower serif of L extends left*   L small, to left

KD   K slightly crooked   Dot above D square on right margin*

KJ   Small dot after J*   K small, central

LA   L smaller   Dot right side of A, L left*

LB   L more central   Oblique line above A of POSTAGE, B left*

LD   Both letters more to right   Oblique line under P of PENNY*

LE   E smaller   Mark in O of POSTAGE*

MD   M to right, D narrower   Mark in N.W. square*

ND   Small dot after D*   D broader, to left

PLATE 50   **PLATE 51**

NL	Small dot after N*	Foot of L slightly longer

OI	Dot on margin under PE of PENNY*	O narrower

OJ	O central	Mark in front of foot of J*

OL	L narrow, lower serif extends left*	O to left

GE

PJ	P smaller	Mark on frame above E of POST-AGE*

QC	C central	Blur in N.E. corner*

R O

RG	G more central	Mark under O of ONE*
RL	R nearly central	R too high and far to left

E   S

SE	Foot of E prolonged*	Mark in corner of S square*

S

SG	S mis-shapen*	G larger
SK	K normal	K cramped, crooked, to left

M

PLATE 50   **PLATE 51**

| TF | F narrow* | F high, far to left |
| TH | H central | H shorter, high |

| TJ | J large, central | Marks bottom of J and in N.W. squares* |
| TK | T central, high | Mark on face, not constant. T high to left |

Unused blocks, including a top half sheet of Plate 50, exist but are scarce, Plate 51 being scarcer than Plate 50. Used examples are fairly plentiful as the stamps were in use from August 1861 to the latter part of 1864. Copies are very often badly off-centre. Clean, well centred, clearly postmarked copies are hard to find.

The first three vertical rows of Plate 51 were badly spaced in the central and lower part of the plate and consequently stamps of these letterings are almost invariably much off-centre. It is exceptional to find well centred stamps from FA–FC down to TA–TC, and the hypothesis put forward for the few well centred copies seen is that the sheet must have been put into the perforating machine upside down.

Plate 50 is slightly more common than Plate 51 in used condition. The number of sheets printed from either is not known but is in the region of 450,000; taking as a guide plates where the total printing is stated.

The colour is normally a deep rose-pink but printings occurred in the pale rose shade in 1863.

These plates reward the beginner by their special interest. They are not too difficult to reconstruct and copies are readily available. They are still fairly cheap and make an attractive display. Recourse to photographs of reconstructed plates should be avoided as it detracts from the interest and reduces the plating to a space-filling operation.

Chapter Six

Fourth Issue of One Penny Perforated

RESERVE PLATES R15 and R16

DIE II: ALPHABET II

These plates were laid down and registered in January 1855, and consequently the check letters are in Alphabet II and the imprimatur sheets were printed on the small crown paper.

Owing to a shortage of the One Penny plates of Type I, and the delay in preparing the plates of the new Type III, these two plates with Plate R17 were put to press in April 1862. The colour was rose-red on the large crown white paper and, as these are the only two plates with Alphabet II in rose-red, they may easily be separated from those in the same colour with Alphabet III, and consequently are as popular for plating as Plates 50 and 51.

These plates were in use during the same period as Plates 50 and 51, although for a slightly shorter time.

Plate R15, of which 221,700 sheets were printed, is somewhat scarcer than Plate R16. The total number printed from Plate R16 is not stated but would be in the region of 350,000. Both plates are known overprinted O.U.S. The stamps are not uncommon.

The identification of the plates is helped by the fact that the check letters on Plate R15 are usually placed very low, whereas those of Plate R16 are placed very high in the corner squares.

Position of Check Letters on Plate R15

Position of Check Letters on Plate R16

ALPHABET II

PLATE R15		PLATE R16	
EK	E low, left; K low, central	Both letters high, central	
EL	Both letters low	E high; L central	
FK	F low; K low, right	Both letters high, central	

PLATE R15		PLATE R16
FL	F low, right; L low, central	F high, central; L high, left
IK	I low, left; K low	I central; K high
IL	I central; L low, left	I right; L right
KK	K low, right; K low, left	Both letters high, central
KL	K low, right; L low, right	K high, right; L slightly right
LK	L low, right; K low, left, inner side of square curved	L high, central; K high
LL	L low, right; L low	L very high; L high, right
MI	M low; I low, left	M high, left; I central
MK	M low, left; K low, right	M high, left; K high, left
ML	M low, central; L low, left	M high, left; L nearly central
SK	s low; K low, right	s high; K high, left
SL	s low; L low, left	s high, central; L high, right

The P's on both plates are usually blind, and the Q's have long horizontal tails.

There are some re-entries on Plate R15, but no noticeable ones on Plate R16 which, however, shows some double letters.

Pl. R15   Pl. R16

RL   LC   MB   MD   TH

DOUBLE LETTERS

The re-entries on Plate R15 are CE, JA, QA, RD and TD.

LE shows a remarkable flaw, probably made in the transferring press. The bottom of the stamp gives evidence of considerable erasure.

Both plates show minor unimportant features, which are given for the purpose of reconstruction and those illustrated are marked with an asterisk (*).

PLATE R15		PLATE R16
AE	Both letters low	Mark above E (? double letter)*
AG⎱	Mark in A square continued*	G higher
BG⎰	to stamp below*	G higher
AK	Marks right of K*	K high
BI	B low, left	Dot above G of POSTAGE*
BJ	Both letters low, left	Top serif of B extends to left*
CK	Both letters low	C very low; K very high
DF	Both letters low	Small diagonal mark in N.W. square*
EF	Marks above F*	F high
EG	E low, left; G lower	Short horizontal mark under G square*
GL	G low, left; L low, right	L touches top of square
HC	Curved mark left of C*	C central
IC	Curved mark left of C; C low	C central
IL	I central	Blob above T of POSTAGE*
JJ	Mark in N.E. square	Both J's central
LC	Both letters low	L double
LE	E corner double*	Both letters higher
MB	M low, left	M double
MD	M low, right	M double
ME	Line under M square*	M high
NI	N low	N very high
OI	O right. Right side of square curved*	O central
PF	P low	Dot on shoulder*
QA	Both letters low. Re-entry	Dot under A
RK	Vertical blur left of K*	R very high, right; K high, left
RL	L double	Both letters high
SH	S very low, left	Horizontal line in S square*
SL	Both letters low	Mark in upper loop of S*
TH	H low, right	T double
TI	T lower	T slightly double
TJ	T lower	T slightly double

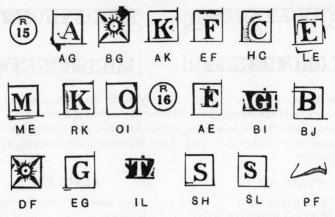

AG	BG	AK	EF	HC	LE
ME	RK	OI	AE	BI	BJ
DF	EG	IL	SH	SL	PF

Plate R16 exhibits a constant mark in the N.W. square on stamps PG, QG, QH, RG, RH, SG, SH, TG and TH which was due to the lodgment of a piece of metal on the roller. This gives a clue as to the method of transferring at this period. The mark consists of a short horizontal line above the nine o'clock ray. There is also a smaller thinner line in conjunction with the more obvious line.

The colour is in a pinkish-red, usually pale and insipid; full pinkish rose-red colours are scarce and printings did not occur in deep rose-red. The plates were not uniformly laid down so that bad centring is a very common feature. Well centred, clean, full colour copies are very scarce, particularly on Plate R15.

These plates are not difficult to reconstruct but a combination of some letters presents difficulty to the beginner, especially the letters E, K, L, M and S; but they present no difficulty when combined with well-defined types. The late J. B. Seymour discovered in Austria many years ago a fine used block from the right-hand half of the sheet containing the K, L and M rows, which finally fixed the few stamps which had been causing difficulty for a long time. The stamp HH of Plate R16 is worth mentioning in this respect. A frequent error is to mark Plate 56 HH as R16. The first H is very high on Plate 56 whereas on R16 neither H is very high. The letter H however should not cause difficulty.

Unused blocks are very rare and those known are not well centred. Used blocks and strips too are scarce and very rare in good well-centred condition.

Chapter Seven

Third and Fourth Issues of Twopence Perforated

THIRD ISSUE: WATERMARK SMALL CROWN

PLATE 4

Plate 4 imperforate was in use over five years, and has been described in Part One.* At this period the wearing of the plate developed rapidly owing to the breaking down of the hardened surface, and the impressions became pitted with spots and patches of colour. This particularly affected the upper part of the stamps in the A horizontal row, and the lower part of the stamps in the T row, causing conspicuous white patches and thickened letters. Repairs were attempted, and the stamps TC and TD are known showing the defective parts restored. The plate, however, was withdrawn as soon as Plate 5 was ready.

The perforated sheets of Plate 4 show the second marginal state only. The bad alignment of the impressions was to some extent responsible for defective perforation.

The 14 perforation came into use for this value at the beginning of March 1855, and as this issue was withdrawn shortly afterwards Plate 4 with this perforation is comparatively scarce.

PLATE 5

Plate 5 was registered in June 1855, and was printed for a short time only on the small crown paper, on which it is an exceedingly scarce stamp. As most of the printing of this plate was carried out on the large crown paper it will be described with Plate 6 in the next issue.

FOURTH ISSUE: WATERMARK LARGE CROWN

PLATES 5 and 6

Plate 5 had been previously registered on the 8th June, 1855 on the small crown paper, and part of that issue appeared simultaneously with both perforations.

Plate 6 was registered on the 11th February, 1857 on the large crown paper and was put to press in May 1857, about the time when Plate 5 was taken from press.

* See Chapter 15, *The Postage Stamps of Great Britain, Part One* (Second Edition), by J. B. Seymour.

The stamps may be easily recognized, as of this value Plate 5 is the only one with Alphabet II, and Plate 6 the only one with Alphabet III. The plates which followed were Type III.

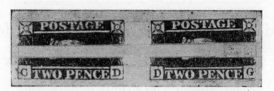

Thick white lines   Thin white lines
Alphabet II   Alphabet III

Further, the white lines on Plate 6 are thinner, but the two alphabets are in most cases an easier and surer means of identification.

The impressions on Plate 5 were badly aligned and most of them lean to the left. The paper was more or less blued, but Plate 6 came into use after the transition period and the paper was generally free from blueing.

All the A's on Plate 5, except MA, are blind.

Perforations 16 and 14 were used for both plates. The 16 gauge was still in use when Plate 5 was put to press; it is rare with this perforation.

In 1857, while Plate 6 was at press, the 16 gauge was again used for a short time. Probably a reserve comb was used in error or to meet an emergency, and examples are almost as scarce as Plate 5 with the same perforation.

Postally used imperforate examples of Plate 5, large crown, are known; they were probably caused by the faulty perforations already described.

The colour of Plate 5 is Prussian blue, with variations, but pale shades are uncommon; Plate 6 is invariably in a deep blue.

RE-ENTRIES

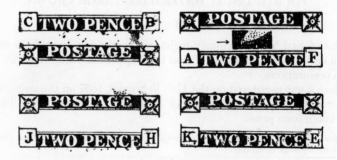

Prominent re-entries on Plates 5 and 6;
CB comes from Plate 5, the remainder from Plate 6

Plate 5. DB is a particularly fine, and the only noticeable re-entry on this plate. It extends above to CB, and is found on the small and large crowns, both with perforations 16 and 14.

Plate 6. shows a sequence of re-entries owing to many of the impressions in the E vertical row having been inaccurately laid down and corrected. The illustrations show that the original impressions of KE to SE were placed too far to the left. Other re-entries on this Plate are AF, JH, and traces on IH.

The late Dr H. Osborne confirmed Plate 6 AF without evidence of fresh entry in used condition. Mr H. F. Johnson later came across the Imprimatur also without the fresh entry. This stamp therefore was re-entered immediately after the onset of printing. To date it is the only copy known.

For an exhaustive survey of these stamps the reader is referred to Dr Osborne's *Twopence Blue Plates 1 to 15.*

DOUBLE LETTERS

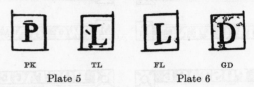

PK   TL   FL   GD

Plate 5   Plate 6

Plate 5. PK, TL. The line over P of PK may be, but possibly is not an indication of a double letter.

Plate 6. FL, GD.

RE-CUT FRAME LINES

Plate 5. The corner squares were not strongly re-cut, and extensions of the frame lines are unusual. The top line on LJ and MI extends to the right.

Plate 6. Many corners were strengthened, and the following may be noted:

The top line extends to left on IJ.

The top line extends to right on EA, EB, FA, HA, IE, GA, RG and TA.

The bottom line extends to right on TI.

The right frame line extends above on FK.

The right frame line extends below on CI, ED, IH, IJ, MG, PI, PJ and QD.

Impressions from both plates are spotted, and show faint smudges which vary, although more or less constant.

CONSTANT MARKS

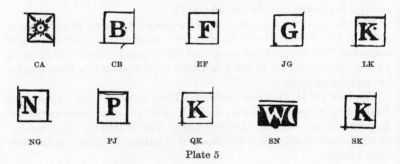

CA   CB   EF   JG   LK

NG   PJ   QK   SN   SK

Plate 5

Plate 5.   CA, dot in N.E. square.

           CB, dot after B.

           CL–DL, marks on margin between the stamps.

           DC, mark over N.W. square.

           EF, horizontal stroke in F square.

FB, dot in E of POSTAGE.

FC, dot above N.E. square, two dots in C.

GB, dots left of and below B.

IJ, mark above OS of POSTAGE.

JE, dot after E.

JG, mark in S.W. corner of G square.

KD, right frame line of S.E. square re-cut.

LK, dot after K.

NG, vertical mark in N square.

PJ, horizontal mark in P square.

QK, dot under the inner corner of K square.

SH, mark in W of TWO.

SK, mark under the inner corner of K square.

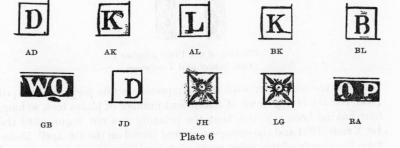

AD   AK   AL   BK   BL

GB   JD   JH   LG   RA

Plate 6

Plate 6. AD, dot in S.E. corner of D square.

AK, mark under the top right serif of K.

AL, mark under L, possibly a double letter.

BC, smudge in C square.

BK, lower right serif of K prolonged.

BL, B broken.

DK, line of dots at side of N.E. square.

FL, mark over F, L double.

GB, strong mark under WO of TWO.

HE, mark under H.

JD, D touches right frame line.

JH, marks outside and in N.W. square (possibly a re-entry).

KH, marks in N.W. square (? re-entry).

LG, large blot in N.E. square.

PD, dot in P.

PK, dot under P.

RA, mark through O and P of TWO PENCE.

RJ, horizontal marks under J and on margin.

SL, blot under L square.

Chapter Eight

Fifth Issue of One Penny Perforated

THE PLATE NUMBERS

Position of the Plate number
One Penny and Twopence

The first transfer roller with seven impressions was prepared in April 1858, but the laying down of a sufficient number of plates took so long, four having been rejected, that the printing was not begun until the 1st March, 1864 and the stamps were first issued on the 1st April. Meantime the supply of this value was maintained from the plates registered in January 1858, supplemented by reserve plates, and there was a reluctance to discard these until they were worn out. The printing was continued by Perkins, Bacon until their contract terminated on the 31st December, 1879.

Plates 69, 70, 75, 77, 126 and 128 were rejected owing to defects or unsuitable spacing for perforation. Plates 226 to 228 were laid down, but were not registered or used. But some stamps from Plate 77 were used, and at least four unused and several used copies are known (*Plate 10*). Alleged copies of Plate 77 on examination usually turn out to be copies taken from Plate 177, with the 1 accidentally or otherwise blotted out. It has been asserted that stamps from Plate 70 have been found, but these usually come from Plate 76, as the small plate numbers were liable to be distorted by imperfect inking, and these supposed copies were not necessarily fraudulent.

Examples of Plate 225, see *Plate 11*, are scarce as it was only four weeks at press, and the very few known unused blocks have realized high prices. Unused examples of Plates 83, 88, 132 and 133 are also scarce, particularly Plate 88.

Used stamps of most of the plates are plentiful, and as the plate

188

number appears on each stamp, the reconstruction of the plates is simple.*

Unused blocks are not scarce and are frequently badly centred, but they are of considerable value with margins showing the plate numbers and inscription. Examples from most of the plates showing these have been found and some complete sheets exist.

Beginning with Plate 88 a serial number was added, and the four plate numbers at the corners of the sheet were enclosed in a circle.

INVERTED WATERMARKS

Examples from every plate probably exist with inverted watermarks, but no complete collection of these is known although some nearly approach it. Only one or two examples are known of some plates and the commonest is from Plate 101. The following list shows the other common examples in their relative order:

Plate 101	Plate 136	Plate 99	Plate 157
Plate 83	Plate 141	Plate 118	Plate 190
Plate 117	Plate 74	Plate 208	Plate 201
Plate 71	Plate 158	Plate 84	

RE-ENTRIES

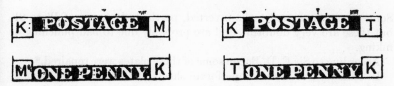

Plate 71

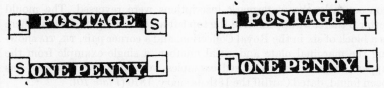

Plate 83

There are few, and the two most noticeable, MK and TK, occur on Plate 71, but good ones occur on SL and TL of Plate 83.

* With the exception of Plate 77, Plates 71 to 225 have been completely reconstructed by one specialist. Ed.

CONSTANT MARKS

Plate 71 shows a thick diagonal cut through the margin between QC and RC, and also incised marks on the Queen's head on NA and RB. Similar marks may be found on other plates, such as on the neck of EC, Plate 76, marks in the upper C square of Plate 73, marks on the E of PENNY and lower margin of AK, Plate 80, and a perpendicular stroke in the lower N square of NA, Plate 94. Some stamps show spots and blotches in the corner squares which are more or less constant, but it is unnecessary to list these as they are not required to identify the plates.

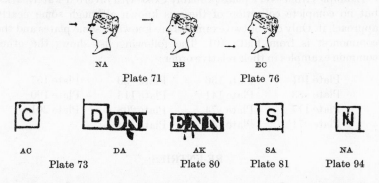

NA   RB   EC
Plate 71   Plate 76

AC   DA   AK   SA   NA
Plate 73   Plate 80   Plate 81   Plate 94

Some S's are supposed to be inverted, particularly on SA of Plate 81, but these are very doubtful, and are probably due to bad punching or inking.

According to Sir E. D. Bacon some of these plates were repaired.*

In January 1870 some imperforate sheets of Plate 116 were sent in error to Cardiff and were sold in the usual way. Probably all the known unused copies come from these, and the variety is known as the 'Cardiff Penny'. The stamps were printed on the wrong side of the paper, and consequently the watermark inscriptions were reversed. The mould letter D therefore appeared in the top left and lower right corners. There is a block of six in the Royal Collection, and a corner pair, TK, TL, showing the marginal plate and serial number; a single example from the upper corner is known. Used examples were unknown, but one has been found, dated Cardiff the 18th January, 1870 (*Plate 10*).

Other known used imperforate examples are:

Plate 79, Newcastle; Limerick.

Plates 81, 86, Newcastle-on-Tyne; London, etc; September/October 1864.

* For details see *Repaired Impressions*, by H. Osborne, M.D.

Plate 88, Manchester; Middlesborough.
Plates 90, 92, 93, 97, Stamford.
Plate 91, Bedale, Yorks; 15th February, 1865.
Plates 100, 102, 103, 104, 105, Brighton.
Plates 107, 108, 109, 114, 117, 120, 121, 122, 136, 146, London.
Plates 148, 158, Edinburgh.
Plates, 162, 164, 171, 174, 191.

Known mint examples are from Plates 107, 120, 122 and 136.
Unused gummed imperforate stamps must not be confused with imprimaturs, which were never gummed.
Single stamps and pieces partly or irregularly perforated may be found.

VARIETIES

Re-entries; Error of watermark MA (ML), to about Plate 96; Inverted watermark.

Plate Number	Series Number	Imprimatur Registered	Put to Press	Earliest Known Date	Sheets Printed
71		14. 3.61	1. 3.64	6. 4.64	557,000
72		14. 3.61	1. 3.64	10. 5.64	522,800
73		14. 3.61	1. 3.64	3. 5.64	529,900
74		14. 3.61	1. 3.64	30. 4.64	531,000
76		7. 2.63	1. 3.64	3. 5.64	555,500
78		7. 2.63	1. 3.64	12. 5.64	615,600
79		7. 2.63	1. 3.64	7. 5.64	638,600
80		7. 2.63	1. 3.64	3. 5.64	495,200
81		7. 2.63	1. 3.64	20. 5.64	520,300
82		1. 3.64	1. 3.64	19. 5.64	263,400
83		1. 3.64	1. 3.64	15. 5.64	199,600
84		1. 3.64	1. 3.64	14. 5.64	369,400
85		1. 3.64	1. 3.64	14. 5.64	510,300
86		1. 3.64	1. 3.64	2. 5.64	460,500
87		7. 3.64	7. 3.64	28. 4.64	462,400
88		17. 3.64	17. 3.64	9. 5.64	199,000
89		22. 3.64	22. 3.64	4. 5.64	503,900
90		30. 3.64	30. 3.64	27. 4.64	471,700
91		5. 4.64	5. 4.64	25. 5.64	384,100
92		12. 4.64	12. 4.64	19. 5.64	567,700
93		19. 4.64	19. 4.64	4. 6.64	455,100
94		26. 4.64	26. 4.64	21. 6.64	478,600
95		14. 6.64	4. 7.64	27. 8.64	533,600
96		5.10.64	11.10.64	6.11.64	488,300
97		5.10.64	7. 3.65	20. 5.65	536,800
98	106	10. 3.65	20. 3.65	23. 5.65	351,400
99	107	5. 1.66	6. 1.66	19. 2.66	355,300
100	110	5. 1.66	19. 1.66	20. 3.66	256,700

Plate Number	Series Number	Imprimatur Registered	Put to Press	Earliest Known Date	Sheets Printed
101	111	5. 1.66	12. 4.66	18. 6.66	372,500
102	112	4. 4.66	16. 4.66	29. 6.66	495,200
103	113	4. 4.66	8. 8.66	9.10.66	400,600
104	114	4. 4.66	22. 1.68	7. 3.68	176,400
105	115	4. 4.66	31. 1.68	3. 2.68	202,600
106	116	4. 4.66	29. 2.68	27. 2.68	391,300
107	117	4. 4.66	18. 3.68	6. 5.68	321,000
108	118	23. 3.68	23. 3.68	28. 5.68	213,500
109	124	23. 3.68	23. 3.68	22. 5.68	236,500
110	125	23. 3.68	23. 3.68	27. 5.68	316,800
111	126	23. 3.68	23. 3.68	7. 5.68	452,700
112	127	12. 5.68	12. 5.68	17. 7.68	299,400
113	128	12. 5.68	12. 5.68	29. 6.68	366,000
114	129	12. 5.68	12. 5.68	10. 7.68	233,100
115	130	12. 5.68	12. 5.68	5. 7.68	214,000
116	131	12. 5.68	12. 5.68	20. 6.68	350,500
117	132	9. 6.68	9. 6.68	31. 7.68	479,000
118	133	9. 6.68	9. 6.68	4. 8.68	440,800
119	134	15. 8.68	18. 8.68	10.10.68	493,800
120	135	15. 8.68	8. 9.68	10.10.68	706,800
121	136	15. 8.68	17.12.68	4. 2.69	406,200
122	137	15. 8.68	16. 1.69	4. 3.69	693,400
123	138	15. 8.68	18. 1.69	2. 3.69	447,800
124	139	15. 8.68	18. 1.69	4. 3.69	597,700
125	140	5. 2.69	15. 2.69	17. 4.69	429,700
127	142	5. 2.69	3. 5.69	28. 6.69	395,300
129	144	5. 2.69	10. 5.69	23. 6.69	434,800
130	145	5. 2.69	5. 6.69	19. 8.69	412,000
131	146	5. 2.69	3. 8.69	16. 9.69	320,700
132	147	5. 2.69	4. 9.69	6.11.69	95,300
133	148	31. 3.69	1.10.69	18.12.69	141,400
134	149	31. 3.69	8.10.69	1. 1.70	793,200
135	150	31. 3.69	13.12.69	15. 2.70	190,500
136	151	1. 3.69	6. 1.70	12. 3.70	299,500
137	153	31. 3.69	5. 3.70	9. 4.70	596,200
138	154	31. 3.69	10. 3.70	15. 4.70	700,300
139	155	2. 2.70	19. 3.70	14. 5.70	194,300
140	156	2. 2.70	9. 4.70	7. 6.70	982,500
141	157	2. 2.70	7. 5.70	6. 6.70	181,300
142	158	2. 2.70	13. 7.70	31. 8.70	212,300
143	160	2. 2.70	7.10.70	14.11.70	286,700
144	161	2. 2.70	3. 1.71	6. 2.71	206,600
145	162	23.12.70	16. 1.71	8. 3.71	545,000
146	163	23.12.70	23. 1.71	25. 3.71	460,100
147	164	23.12.70	4. 2.71	11. 4.71	413,300
148	165	23.12.70	29. 4.71	15. 7.71	507,800
149	166	23.12.70	15. 5.71	7. 7.71	474,900

THE PLATE NUMBERS

[*Plate 9*]

PLATE 77

It is possible to distinguish between Plates 77 and 177 in used copies by
the fact that in Plate 177 none of the upright strokes of the 7's are
placed immediately above the intersection of the curves below. In Plate
77 the left hand 7 is placed immediately above the intersection and the
right hand 7 slightly to the left of the intersection.

PLATE 116

Imperforate: issued at Cardiff in 1870

[*Plate 10*]

PLATE 225

With misplaced vertical perforation

[*Plate 11*]

Plate Number	Series Number	Imprimatur Registered	Put to Press	Earliest Known Date	Sheets Printed
150	167	24. 4.71	30. 5.71	14. 8.71	682,500
151	168	24. 4.71	14.11.71	13.12.71	282,800
152	169	24. 4.71	14.11.71	30.12.71	322,900
153	180	24. 4.71	27.12.71	28. 2.72	128,400
154	181	24. 4.71	30. 1.72	2. 4.72	415,100
155	182	24. 4.71	20. 4.72	15. 6.72	385,300
156	183	12. 1.72	22. 4.72	5. 6.72	496,800
157	184	12. 1.72	22. 4.72	11. 7.72	450,000
158	186	12. 1.72	4. 5.72	11. 7.72	531,000
159	187	12. 1.72	17. 8.72	26.10.72	489,700
160	188	12. 1.72	17. 8.72	4.10.72	525,000
161	191	12. 1.72	17. 9.72	29.11.72	232,300
162	192	24.10.72	26.10.72	6.12.72	365,200
163	194	24.10.72	5.11.72	9. 1.73	377,300
164	195	24.10.72	30.11.72	27. 1.73	318,300
165	196	24.10.72	17. 1.73	10. 3.73	483,300
166	199	24.10.72	18. 1.73	31. 3.73	384,800
167	200	24.10.72	8. 2.73	4. 4.73	497,400
168	201	9. 4.73	8. 5.73	27. 6.73	374,300
169	202	9. 4.73	21. 6.73	8. 9.73	233,100
170	203	9. 4.73	11.10.73	25.11.73	572,500
171	204	9. 4.73	27.10.73	30.12.73	906,700
172	205	9. 4.73	27.10.73	31.12.73	458,600
173	206	9. 4.73	2. 4.74	30. 5.74	303,300
174	207	14.10.73	20. 4.74	10. 7.74	850,000*
175	208	14.10.73	5. 9.74	28.10.74	376,900
176	209	14.10.73	12.12.74	13. 2.75	313,100
177	210	14.10.73	29.12.74	13. 2.75	600,000*
178	211	14.10.73	1. 2.75	5. 4.75	245,600
179	212	14.10.73	15. 5.75	28. 6.75	407,600
180	213	14.10.73	22. 5.75	7. 7.75	215,500
181	214	14.10.73	26. 5.75	22. 7.75	478,600
182	215	13. 4.74	19. 6.75	1. 8.75	215,200
183	216	13. 4.74	9. 8.75	28. 9.75	376,600
184	217	13. 4.74	20.10.75	14. 1.76	300,000*
185	218	13. 4.74	4.12.75	1. 2.76	221,300
186	219	13. 4.74	18.12.75	12. 2.76	304,400
187	222	20. 4.75	3. 1.76	15. 2.76	427,800
188	223	20. 4.75	8. 1.76	4. 3.76	231,600
189	225	20. 4.75	8. 1.76	2. 3.76	218,000
190	226	20. 4.75	31. 1.76	24. 3.76	200,000*
191	228	3. 9.75	19. 2.76	8. 4.76	300,000*
192	229	3. 9.75	19. 2.76	21. 4.76	460,000
193	230	3. 9.75	2. 9.76	3.11.76	350,000*
194	231	3. 9.75	13.11.76	12. 1.77	275,000

* Quantities so marked are estimated.

N

Plate Number	Series Number	Imprimatur Registered	Put to Press	Earliest Known Date	Sheets Printed
195	232	9 . 3 . 76	18 . 11 . 76	8 . 1 . 77	350,000*
196	233	9 . 3 . 76	15 . 1 . 77	7 . 3 . 77	300,000*
197	234	9 . 3 . 76	20 . 1 . 77	7 . 3 . 77	257,200
198	235	9 . 3 . 76	27 . 1 . 77	19 . 3 . 77	300,000*
199	236	9 . 3 . 76	5 . 2 . 77	23 . 3 . 77	314,000
200	237	9 . 3 . 76	3 . 3 . 77	26 . 4 . 77	250,000*
201	238	16 . 11 . 76	21 . 4 . 77	4 . 6 . 77	347,700
202	239	16 . 11 . 76	19 . 5 . 77	21 . 7 . 77	250,000*
203	240	16 . 11 . 76	19 . 5 . 77	19 . 7 . 77	250,000*
204	241	16 . 11 . 76	23 . 6 . 77	13 . 8 . 77	250,000*
205	244	16 . 11 . 76	8 . 9 . 77	27 . 10 . 77	200,000*
206	245	10 . 5 . 77	8 . 9 . 77	7 . 11 . 77	200,000*
207	246	10 . 5 . 77	12 . 11 . 77	20 . 12 . 77	200,000*
208	250	10 . 5 . 77	17 . 11 . 77	25 . 1 . 78	150,000*
209	251	10 . 5 . 77	24 . 11 . 77	1 . 1 . 78	150,000*
210	252	16 . 11 . 77	8 . 12 . 77	6 . 2 . 78	189,100
211	253	16 . 11 . 77	16 . 3 . 78	16 . 3 . 78	50,000*
212	254	16 . 11 . 77	20 . 5 . 78	10 . 7 . 78	100,000*
213	255	25 . 2 . 78	1 . 7 . 78	5 . 9 . 78	90,000*
214	256	25 . 2 . 78	6 . 8 . 78	20 . 9 . 78	80,000*
215	257	25 . 2 . 78	6 . 8 . 78	14 . 10 . 78	80,000*
216	258	25 . 2 . 78	2 . 9 . 78	28 . 10 . 78	90,000*
217	259	14 . 8 . 78	23 . 11 . 78	17 . 1 . 79	80,000*
218	260	14 . 8 . 78	30 . 11 . 78	31 . 12 . 78	50,000*
219	261	14 . 8 . 78	11 . 1 . 79	21 . 2 . 79	45,000*
220	262	14 . 8 . 78	11 . 1 . 79	17 . 2 . 79	80,000*
221	263	31 . 12 . 78	3 . 4 . 79	26 . 5 . 79	60,000*
222	264	31 . 12 . 78	6 . 5 . 79	26 . 6 . 79	50,000*
223	265	31 . 12 . 78	21 . 6 . 79	22 . 8 . 79	50,000*
224	267	31 . 12 . 78	23 . 6 . 79	4 . 9 . 79	45,000*
225	268	31 . 12 . 78	27 . 10 . 79	4 . 12 . 79	25,000*

* Quantities so marked are estimated.

PROTECTIVE OVERPRINTS

Before the introduction of Postal Orders in 1881, it was customary to remit small payments in postage stamps, which could be cashed at any post office. This practice was open to petty pilfering, and in 1867 firms, in order to protect themselves, asked to have their stamps marked in a way which would render them non-negotiable.

In 1859 the Oxford Union Society printed their initials on the face of the stamps provided, free of charge, in their writing rooms which franked the letters of their members. This was continued without objection until 1869.

To meet the business firms' requirements, the postal authorities in 1867 agreed to print the firm's name on the back of the stamps, before gumming, and for this purpose instructed Perkins, Bacon to prepare for use when required formes consisting of 240 stereos at a cost of £5 plus 5s. per hundred sheets for printing.*

The Oxford Union Society was informed that it would require to comply with this method, and that overprinting on the face of the stamps would no longer be permitted. A new and wider setting of the overprint was prepared, and the stamps, printed on the back, continued in use until the privilege was withdrawn in 1882.

The only firms who availed themselves of the concession were J. & C. Boyd, W. H. Smith & Son, Copestake, Moore, Crampton & Co., and the Great Eastern Railway.

This method of protection was superseded by the authorities approving J. Sloper & Co's patent, by which a firm's initials could be perforated through the stamps, and this method is still adopted. These privately perforated stamps have no philatelic value. In 1896 the late B. McGowan compiled a useful list of the overprints, which was published in the *British Philatelist*.

1. *Oxford Union Society*

A. o.u.s. in block type, between narrow wavy lines; printed in vermilion on the face of the stamps; 1859 to 1870.

1d Type I. Watermark large crown; rose-red.
Plates 27, 36, 39, 42, 43, 46, 47, 48, 50, 52, 55 to 60, 66, R15, R16.

1d Type III. Plates 71 to 74, 76, 78 to 107, 109 to 119, 121, 123, 125, 129 to 135, 137, 139, 140, 142.

B. o.u.s., between lines wider apart; printed in vermilion on the back of the stamps, before gumming; 1873 to 1879.

1d Type III. Plates 119, 124, 130, 134, 135, 136, 143, 146, 150, 155, 156, 159, 160, 162 to 166, 169, 170, 171, 174, 177, 179, 180, 182, 183, 185, 197, 199, 204, 205, 208, 212, 213, 215, 218.

The overprints normally read upwards, but owing to the inversion of some sheets they may be found reading downwards. Examples are known with no stop after the o, and with double overprints.

These stamps normally have the Oxford (603) duplex cancellation, of

* See also *Perkins, Bacon Records*, Vol. II, pp. 540 to 564.

which several types exist. Stamps of the fourth issue are usually cancelled with the obliteration of the London City type, and a similar, but
narrower, type was also used. Further, these stamps and the early plates
of the Fifth Issue are found with the larger obliteration (Fig. 59).*
Later, a four-bar upright postmark was generally used, and about 1870 a
narrower form of this type appeared with small figures and a round-
topped 3, and also with taller figures and a flat-topped 3. The two types
are frequently found with the error 613 for 603.

At the beginning of 1880 a narrower overprint was again used, but
printed in carmine over the gum. This is found on the One Penny
venetian red and on the One Penny lilac (14 and 16 dots). An overprint
in violet on these issues also exists but neither of these has any official
status, as evidently they were privately printed.

J. & C. Boyd & Co., 7 Friday St., 1867

J. & C.
BOYD & CO.
7 FRIDAY ST.

Printed in three lines under the gum, in the colour of the stamp.

1d Type III. Plates 73, 74, 78, 79, 85, 87, 90, 102, 103, 107, 108, 111,
112, 113, 115, 118 to 121, 124, 127, 129, 130, 132, 133, 134, 139,
140, 143, 145, 146, 148, 150, 152, 154, 155, 159, 160, 162 to 167,
170, 171, 172, 177, 179, 181, 183, 185, 187, 192 to 195, 198, 199,
205, 206, 207, 209, 213, 224.
Plate 139 is known unused.
2d Type III. Plates 9, 13.

Stamps exist with a similar overprint in different type, but printed
over the gum. These were privately done, and have no official standing.
The One Penny Plate 90 exists unused.

Copestake, Moore, Crampton & Co., London, 1867

COPESTAKE,
MOORE,
CRAMPTON, & CO.,
London.

Printed in four lines under the gum in the colour of the stamp.

* See Part One (second edition), p. 27.

A. 1d Type III. Plates 74, 76, 78, 79, 80, 90, 92, 96, 97, 100 to 120,
122, 123, 125, 127, 129, 130, 131, 132 to 150, 152, 154, 155, 157,
158, 160, 162, 163, 164, 167, 168, 169, 171, 172, 174 to 181, 183,
185 to 189, 191, 192, 194, 196 to 202, 204 to 207, 211, 213, 214,
215, 219, 224.

1½d Type V. Plates 1, 3.

2d Type III. Plates 9, 12 to 15.

B. Sans-serif letters; printed in four lines, in vermilion;
½d Type IV. Plates 3 to 6, 8 to 15, 20.

COPESTAKE,
MOORE,
CRAMPTON,
& CO.,
LONDON.

C. On the surface printed stamps, printed by De La Rue & Co. Overprinted in sans-serif type, in five lines in the colour of the
stamps.

1d Venetian red.

3d Rose; Plates 5, 8, 14, 18, 19, 20.

6d Violet. Plates 8, 9.

6d Grey. Plate 14.

1s Green. Plates 4, 12.

There are various private overprints used by this firm, in four lines
over the gum. They are usually in black, but may be found in colour.
A vertical overprint exists, printed in colour in five lines, which reads
'Copestake, Hughes, Crampton & Co., London'.

W. H. Smith & Son, 186, Strand

W. H. SMITH
AND SON,
186, STRAND.

Printed in three lines in red, under the gum, 1867:

1d Type III. Plates 73, 78, 92, 97, 102, 103, 109, 111, 114, 119,
121, 124, 131, 134, 147, 152, 164, 169, 173, 174, 183.

2d Type III. Printed in blue; Plates 9, 10. Proofs or essays exist
with various types of the print in blue-black, green, and red,
on the face and back of the stamps.

Great Eastern Railway

G. E. R.

G.E.R. printed horizontally in red, under the gum, 1873.
1d Type III. Plates 95, 111, 124, 134, 149, 151, 155 to 158, 163, 168, 171, 174, 175, 178, 181, 184, 185, 189.

Although few firms availed themselves of the privilege of having their names officially printed on the stamps, many others had them privately printed over the gum. Of these the best known are:

> Barrowman, Phillips & Co.
> Cocker Brothers Ltd., Sheffield.
> Wm. Dawbarn & Co., Liverpool.
> The Fore Street Warehouse Co., Ltd.
> G. H. W. & Co., St. Pauls.
> G. S. S. & Co.
> James Harvey, B. Stortford.
> A. S. Henry & Co., Glasgow.
> Holloway, 264.
> Samuel Montague & Co.
> J. Taylor & Sons, Newgate St.
> Vickers, Sons & Co., Sheffield.

Chapter Nine

Fifth Issue of Twopence Perforated

THE PLATE NUMBERS

July, 1858; Plates 7 to 9, 12; with thick white lines.
7th July, 1869; Plates 13 to 15; with thinner white lines.

After the printing had begun on the 19th July, 1858 a circular was sent to all postmasters informing them of the new design, which was issued at once. Apparently the printing from one plate was at first sufficient to meet the demand. Nine plates were laid down between June 1858 and September 1875, but Plates 10 and 11 were rejected as the impressions were inaccurately laid down.

Examples from Plates 7, 8 and 12 are scarce, and rare in mint condition, but Plate 9 is common. A different roller impression was used for Plates 13 to 15, and these show few interesting features. Stamps from Plate 15 exist in a deeper and richer blue. The new serial numbers and the added circle to the plate numbers began with Plate 12.

This value also shows blurs, blotches, and scratches in the corner squares or on the margin, but it is unnecessary to detail these.

NG   JL

Plate 7. The stamp JL appears to show a double J in the N.E. corner, and there are distinct marks in ST of POSTAGE on NG.

AK   LB   TH

Plate 8. On AK there is a well-defined mark on the head, and also between AL/BL. On DA and KB there is a mark in the white line above TWO PENCE, in the G of POSTAGE on LB, and the O of TWO on TH.

199

| AH | BH | IB | KJ |

Plate 9. There are distinct marks above and on NC of PENCE on AH, and below, and in GE of POSTAGE on BH. There is a dot in the lower B of IB, and a line through the N of PENCE and the white line above it on KJ.

NL

Plate 12. NL shows a line through the diadem and hair.

RE-ENTRIES

Most of these occur on Plate 7 and some of these are unusual, as the double impressions show not only at the top or bottom of the stamps, but throughout the whole design, and frequently disfigure the Queen's head, as shown on HG.

HG

The more interesting are AG, AH, BB/CB, DC/EC, FB/GB, HG/IG, JB/KB and NB/OB.

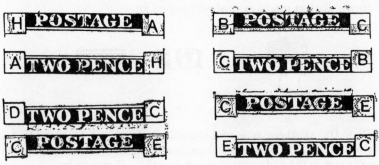

Plate 7

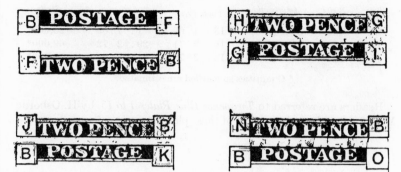

Plate 7

Those on Plates 8 and 9 are not conspicuous, but traces are found on a few impressions from Plate 8, particularly on DA, RE and TH.

AA and AB, Plate 12, are strong re-entries.

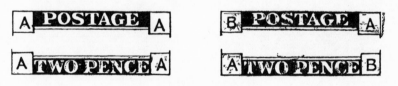

Plate 12

VARIETIES

Inverted watermarks; Ivory heads; Imperforate, Plate 9, used at Greenock; Imperforate, Plate 13.

The imperforate examples of Plate 13 on experimental paper are liable to be confused with the issued variety.

The paper for both values was normally white, and being hand-made, varied from very thin to thick. Some printings, however, show decided blueings, and Ivory Heads sometimes occur.

The MA (ML) watermark error is now known to exist on this value.

Examples showing damaged crowns have been noted, and may also be found on the penny value.

Plate Number	Series Number	Imprimatur Registered	Put to Press	Earliest Known Date	Sheets Printed
7	—	11 . 6 . 58	19 . 7 . 58	July '58	40,000
8	—	7 . 7 . 59	21 . 9 . 59	30 . 9 . 59	66,000
9	—	14 . 3 . 61	14 . 3 . 61	14 . 5 . 61	383,500
12	123	1 . 1 . 68	28 . 10 . 68	22 . 12 . 68	30,600

Plate Number	Series Number	Imprimatur Registered	Put to Press	Earliest Known Date	Sheets Printed
13	152	31 . 3 . 69	13 . 4 . 69	1 . 7 . 69	125,000
14	170	24 . 4 . 71	16 . 9 . 71	29 . 2 . 72	69,000*
15	227	3 . 9 . 75	14 . 3 . 76	21 . 8 . 76	90,000*

* Quantities so marked are estimated.

Readers are referred to *Twopence Blue Plates 1 to 15*, by H. Osborne M.D. for an exhaustive survey of these plates.

Chapter Ten

The Halfpenny and Three Halfpence

THE HALFPENNY

The watermark extended over three stamps, and the details regarding the die, mould figures, and marginal inscription, etc, have been described in Part One.

Position of Plate numbers

This value was introduced on account of the reduced rate for newspapers, and other printed matter. The issue was announced to take effect on the 1st October, 1870 by a post office circular dated the 10th September, 1870.

The sheets contained 480 stamps in 20 horizontal rows of 24, and the check letters run from

AA	XA		AT	XT
—		to		—
AA	AX		TA	TX

This value was in use for nine years, and Plates 1, 3 to 6, 8 to 15, 19 and 20 were put to press. Plates 2, 7, 16, 17, 18 were not completed, and Plates 21 and 22 were laid down but not used. Plate 9 is the only scarce one, as it was kept in reserve for emergencies and was not often put to press. Unlike the previous values, the sheets were perforated vertically. The comb contained 21 rows of pins and, as only 24 rows were perforated, the side of the final row, A or X, was imperforate, according to the way in which the sheet was placed on the machine.

The One Penny and Twopence always show a perforated top or bottom margin. Examples of the Halfpenny are known showing perforations on a side margin owing to some sheets having received an extra row.

Stamps from Plates 1, 4, 5, 6, 8 and 14 are known imperforate, some of which are due to rows having been missed in perforating; these exist on entries.

Pairs are also known imperforate between. These, however, must not be confused with the proofs and colour trials. The colour is rose-red, showing shades, and the paper is free from blueing.

Mint examples are not common, and corner blocks with the marginal details are scarce, but examples of each plate are known, including the rare Plate 9, of which a corner block of 72 is in the Royal collection. A used block of 18 is also known.

VARIETIES

Imperforate; Plates 1, 4, 5, 6, 8, 14.
Watermark inverted.
Watermark reversed.
No watermark, due to faulty registration or badly cut paper.

Plate Number	Series Number	Imprimatur Registered	Put to Press	Earliest Known Date	Sheets Printed
1	171	20 . 6 . 70	20 . 6 . 70	1 . 10 . 70	121,500
3	173	28 . 6 . 70	28 . 6 . 70	1 . 10 . 70	192,500
4	174	4 . 7 . 70	4 . 7 . 70	15 . 10 . 70	264,600
5	175	19 . 7 . 70	12 . 7 . 70	24 . 10 . 70	533,200
6	176	19 . 7 . 70	19 . 7 . 70	19 . 10 . 70	402,100
8	177	26 . 7 . 70	?	31 . 10 . 70	120,000*
9	178	23 . 12 . 70	9 . 10 . 71	5 . 12 . 71	50,000*
10	197	24 . 10 . 72	2 . 10 . 73	22 . 12 . 73	386,100
11	198	24 . 10 . 72	21 . 1 . 74	4 . 6 . 74	411,000
12	220	13 . 4 . 74	29 . 6 . 74	28 . 8 . 74	400,000*
13	221	20 . 4 . 75	6 . 5 . 76	27 . 6 . 76	300,000*
14	224	30 . 4 . 75	16 . 11 . 76	9 . 3 . 77	250,000*
15	242	16 . 11 . 76	6 . 5 . 78	10 . 7 . 78	200,000*
19	248	16 . 11 . 77	18 . 7 . 78	23 . 8 . 78	175,000*
20	249	31 . 12 . 78	27 . 6 . 79	4 . 10 . 79	150,000*

* Estimated number of sheets printed.

THREE HALFPENCE

Position of Plate number

This value was introduced on account of a proposed change in the postal rates, and Plate 1 was registered on the 22nd March, 1860 in lilac-rose. 10,000 sheets were printed on the Type 1 large crown paper, and were gummed and perforated at Somerset House. The paper showed considerable blueing. As the proposed rate failed to secure parliamentary sanction the stock of about 8962 sheets, according to Wright and Creeke, was destroyed in May 1867.

About 1000 sheets overprinted SPECIMEN had already been distributed, mainly to postmasters, and a few preserved sheets have since been cut up, and examples are in the possession of collectors. Used examples are unknown.

Ten years later new rates, including this value, were introduced for printed matter on the 1st October, 1870, and Plate 1 was again put to press on the Type 2 large crown paper. The colour was changed to lake-red. 66,134 sheets were so printed.

Plate 2 was defective and not completed, and Plate 3 was laid down at the end of 1871. It was, however, not registered until April 1874, and produced 123,500 sheets from the 10th August, 1874 to the end of 1879. The line-engraved issues were superseded in October 1880 by the issues surface-printed by De La Rue.

Though Plates 1 and 3 were made from the same die, and show the same marginal inscriptions, they differ in other respects. The stamps from Plate 1 do not show the plate number, whereas it appears on Plate 3, which was laid down from a new transfer roller.

The marginal corner plate numbers on Plate 1 are unenclosed, and it has no serial number, while on Plate 3 the corner numbers are within a circle, and it shows the serial number 193. The dividing star on Plate 1 is Type B2, and on Plate 3, Type B1.

Type B1 Type B2
Plate 3 Plate 1

The error of lettering, OP over PC for CP over PC on Plate 1 occurs on all printings. Probably it was not noticed, and consequently not corrected. It was first pointed out in an American journal in December, 1894.

Used and unused imperforate examples from both plates exist, and are very rare. Imperforate examples of Plate 1 on blued paper were experimental, and not issued.

Stamps from Plate 1 are less common than Plate 3, and mint examples are becoming scarce. The OP–PC error has lately much increased in value, and mint copies are very rare. It exists in two mint blocks of nine and twelve stamps, and has also been found in a used block of six. The only known example in lilac-rose is in the Royal Collection. Examples from both plates may be found with inverted watermark.

Appendix

One Penny Plate Varieties

DIE II : ALPHABETS II, III and IV

R : Re-entries, Fresh Entries, Coincident Re-entries
D : Double Letters
V : Other Varieties

AA	R	30, 42, 55		AK	R	41
	D				D	1
	V	33, 41, 47, 50, 51			V	7, 10, 13, 30, 32, 52, 55, 58,
AB	R	41				59, 60, 62, R15, R16
	D			AL	R	
	V	9, 14, 16, 21, 44, 47, 52, 56,			D	9, 41, 48
		61			V	1, 6, 23, 27, 32, 47, 62, 67
AC	R	30, 41		BA	R	41, 55
	D				D	
	V	11, 41, 42, 43, 44, 49, 66			V	12, 14, 26, 28, 29, 33, 38,
AD	R	27, 41, 49				41, 44, 49, 50, 51, 52, 61,
	D	5				66, 68
	V	44, 60		BB	R	41
AE	R	41			D	
	D				V	6, 33, 41, 43, 44, 48, 49, 50,
	V	3, 5, 7, 21, 47, 49, 50, 51,				51, 56, 57, 59
		56, 58, 62, R15, R16		BC	R	41
AF	R				D	
	D	13			V	4, 9, 12, 16, 30, 32, 33, 38,
	V	16, 41, 49, 55				41, 49, 50, 51, 56, 62, 66
AG	R	41, 68		BD	R	27, 41
	D				D	
	V	1, 5, 16, 41, 43, 47, 55, 59,			V	4, 10, 21, 32, 41, 47, 58
		R15, R16		BE	R	41, 62
AH	R	41			D	
	D	47			V	41, 47, 49, 50, 51, 59, R17
	V	2, 20, 27, 34, 48, 49		BF	R	41
AI	R	41			D	40
	D				V	2, 13, 16, 21, 36, 40, 41, 42,
	V	6, 7, 8, 13, 42, 47, 48, 58,				43, 47, 49, 52, 57, 58, 59,
		59				62, 67
AJ	R	41		BG	R	32, 41, 48
	D				D	
	V	11, 13, 15, 41, 50, 51, 52,			V	1, 13, 15, 39, 41, 42, 47, 49,
		55				52, 68, R15, R16

BH R 41, 46
    D
    V 7, 8, 15, 19, 41, 42, 55, 58,
       59, 62

BI R 2, 37, 41, 60
    D 35
    V 7, 13, 27, 41, 48, 52, 57, 59,
       63, 66, 68, R15, R16

BJ R 41, 57
    D 29
    V 5, 6, 9, 13, 41, 42, 45, 49,
       50, 51, 52, 59, R15, R16

BK R 41
    D
    V 36, 41, 46, 52, 55, 59, 66

BL R 41
    D 37
    V 4, 5, 13, 20, 27, 32, 38, 41,
       49, 50, 51, 55, 57, 59, 62

CA R 41, 55
    D
    V 14, 49, 56

CB R 41
    D
    V 28, 49, 50, 51, 58

CC R 41
    D
    V 15, 23, 47, 49

CD R 41
    D 58
    V 44, 49, 50, 51, 60

CE R 22, 41, R15
    D 30
    V 2, 16, 44, 49, 56, 58

CF R 41
    D
    V 16, 23, 43, 45, 49, 57, 66

CG R 41
    D
    V 8, 14, 44, 49, 60

CH R 41
    D
    V 39, 44, 46, 49, 52, 64

CI R 41, 59
    D
    V 1, 2, 6, 8, 44, 50, 51

CJ R 41
    D
    V 5, 9, 10, 13, 52, 55, 58, 59

CK R 41
    D
    V 2, 5, 12, 17, 36, 41, 42, 52,
       55, 58, 59, 67, R15, R16

CL R 61
    D
    V 1, 5, 9, 10, 14, 16, 20, 41,
       49, 55, 56, 59, 66

DA R 41, 55
    D
    V 1, 6, 36, 37, 57, 66

DB R 41, 55
    D
    V 16, 60, 67

DC R 41
    D
    V 9, 36, 47, 48

DD R 41
    D
    V 4, 6, 9, 16, 39, 52, 57, 60

DE R 41
    D
    V 3, 16, 34, 49, 50, 51, 60, 65

DF R 41
    D
    V 16, 34, 56, R15, R16

DG R 41, 56
    D
    V 6, 12, 36, 39, 43, 50, 51, 55,
       58

DH R 41
    D
    V 15, 48, 49, 52, 58, 59

DI R 41
    D
    V 27, 43, 47, 50, 51, 52, 55,
       59, 62

DJ R 41
    D R17
    V 5, 7, 20, 43, 58, 59, 62

DK R 41
    D
    V 12, 13, 31, 36, 37, 39, 52,
       55, 58, 59, 67

DL R 41, 61
    D
    V 5, 6, 10, 12, 13, 16, 19, 20,
       23, 43, 47, 59

EA	R	
	D	
	V	4, 5, 37, 48, 52, 64, 66
EB	R	
	D	
	V	5, 7, 16, 34, 43, 44, 50, 51, 56, 58, 60, 67
EC	R	
	D	47
	V	2, 7, 15, 34, 47, 48, 59
ED	R	
	D	
	V	9, 19, 56, 57
EE	R	
	D	
	V	2, 59, 64
EF	R	24
	D	39
	V	16, 50, 51, 56, R15, R16
EG	R	
	D	
	V	2, 5, 6, 7, 9, 10, 31, 34, 52, 55, 58, 59, 61, R15, R16
EH	R	6
	D	57
	V	1, 14, 16, 43, 48, 52, 55, 58, 59, 62, 64, 66
EI	R	
	D	
	V	16, 41, 43, 62, 64
EJ	R	
	D	
	V	4, 39, 58, 59, 60
EK	R	24
	D	59
	V	5, 27, 34, 43, 49, 52, 55, 58, R15, R16
EL	R	61
	D	
	V	3, 6, 7, 10, 20, 23, 46, 49, 52, 56, 58, 67, R15, R16
FA	R	
	D	
	V	5, 7, 34, 39, 42, 48, 49, 66, 68
FB	R	55, 60
	D	
	V	1, 5, 6, 9, 14, 52, 58, 61, 67

FC	R	
	D	60
	V	7, 8, 9, 14, 50, 51, 52
FD	R	
	D	
	V	14, 50, 51, 59, 60, 62
FE	R	
	D	
	V	4, 41, 43, 44, 57, 66
FF	R	
	D	
	V	1, 7, 9, 41, 55, 56, 66
FG	R	31
	D	5
	V	2, 6, 7, 20, 39, 42, 56, 58, 59
FH	R	
	D	
	V	1, 5, 11, 55, 56, 58
FI	R	
	D	
	V	4, 6, 7, 22, 34, 37, 46, 55, 58, 62
FJ	R	27
	D	
	V	5, 45, 58, 59
FK	R	24, 25, 27
	D	64
	V	5, 6, 12, 13, 16, 44, 55, 67, R15, R16
FL	R	61
	D	
	V	5, 6, 12, 20, 32, 44, 48, 49, 55, 60, R15, R16
GA	R	
	D	
	V	5, 15, 44, 49, 57, 67
GB	R	
	D	
	V	5, 7, 17, 37, 43, 49, 50, 51, 52, 56, 58, 67
GC	R	
	D	60
	V	10, 34, 52, 67, 68
GD	R	
	D	48
	V	7, 34, 45, R17

O

GE	*R*	
	D	46
	V	2, 3, 6, 22, 39, 50, 51, 56, 63
GF	*R*	
	D	31
	V	55, 56, 63
GG	*R*	39
	D	
	V	5, 6, 9, 10, 16, 21, 39, 49, 55, 59, 62
GH	*R*	
	D	
	V	4, 9, 34, 36, 39, 52, 62
GI	*R*	31
	D	
	V	3, 5, 7, 46, 62
GJ	*R*	56
	D	
	V	39, 52
GK	*R*	
	D	34
	V	5, 11, 28, 36, 39, 44, 55, 59, 62, 67
GL	*R*	28, 61
	D	48
	V	3, 12, 58, 62, R15, R16
HA	*R*	
	D	4
	V	2, 10, 46, 47, 49, 50, 51, 56, 58, 66
HB	*R*	
	D	5
	V	11, 12, 16, 44, 56, 58, 59
HC	*R*	
	D	
	V	45, 46, 56, 59, 60, R15, R16
HD	*R*	40, 55
	D	
	V	7, 9, 46, 56
HE	*R*	
	D	
	V	2, 4, 44, 56, 58, 61
HF	*R*	
	D	
	V	2, 4, 44, 50, 51, 55, 56, 57, 60

HG	*R*	
	D	
	V	3, 6, 9, 14, 16, 27, 47, 55, 56, 57, 58
HH	*R*	
	D	10
	V	1, 20, 34, 52, 56, 57
HI	*R*	46
	D	22
	V	7, 9, 11, 12, 58, 59
HJ	*R*	57
	D	
	V	16, 52, 55, 59, 62
HK	*R*	
	D	57
	V	7, 8, 11, 14, 31, 37, 52, 55, 62
HL	*R*	28, 61
	D	60
	V	6, 17, 42, 49, 52, 55, 56, 57, 58
IA	*R*	3
	D	
	V	2, 47, 58
IB	*R*	
	D	
	V	2, 3, 6, 7, 17, 18, 49, 50, 51, 59, 60
IC	*R*	
	D	
	V	2, 5, 7, 17, 34, 48, 52, 56, R15, R16
ID	*R*	
	D	
	V	6, 39, 44, 56, 58, 59
IE	*R*	25, 68
	D	
	V	12, 15, 49, 56, 57, 59, 63, 68
IF	*R*	68
	D	
	V	3, 39, 47, 52, 59, 62
IG	*R*	9
	D	
	V	1, 16, 52, 56
IH	*R*	
	D	42, 52, 55, 62, 67
	V	6

	R	D	V
II			9, 12, 16, 52, 55
IJ			10, 21, 50, 51, 52
IK			5, 6, 8, 10, 16, 42, 43, 55, 57, R15, R16
IL	61		4, 6, 7, 55, 61, R15, R16
JA	R15		5, 7, 10, 17, 27, 33, 50, 51, 52, 67
JB			6, 7, 10, 27, 36, 48
JC			4, 27, 52, 56
JD			5, 8, 34, 43, 44, 49, 50, 51, 52, 56
JE	68		56, 57
JF	68, R17		55, 56, 58, 60, 63
JG			1, 2, 7, 8, 10, 52, 55, 68
JH			4, 6, 7, 9, 10, 16, 39, 47, 52, 59
JI		56	1, 4, 5, 6, 8, 9, 44, 52
JJ		66	5, 15, 36, 41, 42, 52, 59, R15, R16
JK			28, 52, 55, 56, 58, 61
JL	61		10, 19, 36, 47, 48, 49, 50, 51, 57, 58
KA			6, 32, 42, 68
KB			2, 6, 7, 11, 16, 30, 34, 39, 47
KC	23, 33		9, 34, 37, 49, 56, 57
KD		37, 40, 45	20, 25, 49, 50, 51, 56, 58
KE		40, 43	21, 28, 35, 56, 68
KF			6, 23, 25, 27, 47, 49, 56, 57
KG		55	1, 6, 20, 49, 56
KH		40	5, 6, 26, 32, 34, 37, 45, 48, 56, 62
KI	28		3, 5, 7, 12, 29, 44, 48, 52, 56, 63
KJ		40	9, 16, 24, 27, 33, 38, 49, 50, 51, 52, 60, 62
KK	10		12, 13, 17, 20, 28, 37, 49, 52, 63, 68, R15, R16
KL	10, 61, 68	25, 58	27, 28, 39, 57, 59, 61, 63, R15, R16

LA   R   3
    D
    V   1, 2, 10, 36, 44, 49, 50, 51, 56, 58, 63, 67

LB   R
    D
    V   7, 36, 45, 49, 50, 51, 52, 56

LC   R   55
    D   R16
    V   3, 6, 8, 56, R15

LD   R
    D   35, 40, 45
    V   1, 4, 8, 14, 16, 20, 34, 37, 48, 50, 51, 56, 58

LE   R   28
    D
    V   6, 28, 34, 41, 49, 50, 51, 56, 63, 67, R15, R16

LF   R
    D
    V   5, 6, 32, 34, 37, 42, 47, 56, 58, 61, 64

LG   R
    D   58, 61, 68
    V   1, 25, 29, 34, 49, 55, 58

LH   R
    D   42, 47
    V   6, 19, 31, 45, 52, 58, 61, 62

LI   R   46, 61
    D   45
    V   36, 43, 47, 58, 61

LJ   R   5
    D   43
    V   6, 10, 12, 16, 18, 24, 40, 48, 52, 58, 59

LK   R   62
    D
    V   5, 6, 7, 10, 12, 29, 46, 49, 52, 56, 58, 68, R15, R16

LL   R
    D   40
    V   5, 6, 24, 27, 35, 37, 43, 47, 55, 58, 61, R15, R16

MA   R
    D
    V   2, 5, 9, 31, 42, 44, 46, 49, 58

MB   R   55
    D   R16
    V   4, 7, 16, 56, 62, 67, R15

MC   R
    D
    V   8, 10, 14, 36, 39, 40, 46, 56

MD   R
    D   R16
    V   1, 9, 14, 16, 41, 43, 50, 51, 56, R15

ME   R
    D
    V   9, 16, 29, 35, 37, 40, 41, 56, 60, 63, R15, R16

MF   R   28
    D
    V   6, 7, 13, 44, 48, 49, 62

MG   R
    D
    V   1, 5, 16, 24, 27, 30, 42, 47, 49, 52, 56, 58, 61, 62

MH   R
    D
    V   1, 6, 23, 26, 35, 36, 37, 44, 46, 55, 58, 61, 64

MI   R
    D   44
    V   5, 42, 45, 46, 49, 58, 66, R15, R16

MJ   R   5, 34
    D
    V   12, 19, 30, 32, 34, 40, 45, 55, 58, 61

MK   R
    D
    V   13, 14, 16, 32, 40, 44, 52, 55, 58, 61, 62, R15, R16

ML   R   61
    D   40, 57.
    V   1, 13, 29, 40, 42, 43, 46, 49, 55, 58, 59, R15, R16

NA   R
    D
    V   7, 36, 46, 52

NB   R
    D   37
    V   9, 11, 14, 28, 42, 43, 44, 49, 56, 59

NC   R   68
    D
    V   2, 7, 8, 13, 37, 40, 43, 45, 49, 52, 56, 58, 60

ND	R	
	D	
	V	1, 3, 16, 31, 45, 49, 50, 51, 56, 58, 60, 61, 62
NE	R	
	D	
	V	1, 5, 9, 14, 16, 35, 56
NF	R	
	D	30
	V	7, 28, 36, 49, 52, 59, 62
NG	R	16, 58
	D	
	V	2, 7, 8, 43, 58, 61, 62
NH	R	
	D	
	V	10, 12, 34, 40, 44, 47, 58, 59, 61, 62
NI	R	29, 56
	D	
	V	3, 6, 37, 44, 48, 52, 62, 66, R15, R16
NJ	R	
	D	
	V	8, 13, 19, 29, 33, 44, 49, 55, 62
NK	R	31
	D	
	V	23, 31, 33, 36, 37, 47, 55, 57, 58, 61
NL	R	28
	D	
	V	5, 10, 44, 46, 50, 51, 55, 58, 62
OA	R	
	D	
	V	4, 20, 30, 36, 38, 43, 48, 49
OB	R	34
	D	
	V	8, 16, 42, 49, 57, 58, 59, 62
OC	R	55, 60
	D	39
	V	7, 44, 45, 46, 49, 58, 67
OD	R	
	D	23
	V	15, 16, 34, 36, 44, 46, 49, 58, 61, R17
OE	R	14, 16
	D	R17
	V	3, 6, 8, 17, 19, 42, 52, 56, 57, 58, 61

OF	R	
	D	
	V	1, 3, 6, 10, 28, 31, 47, 52, 58, 60, 61
OG	R	
	D	R17
	V	2, 6, 7, 9, 16, 20, 31, 37, 38, 49, 52, 58, R17
OH	R	
	D	
	V	24, 48, 52, 55, 58
OI	R	29, 56
	D	45
	V	3, 10, 20, 35, 44, 48, 49, 50, 51, 52, 58, 59, 61, R15, R16
OJ	R	
	D	
	V	1, 5, 8, 10, 41, 46, 47, 50, 51, 52, 56, 58, 61, 63, 64
OK	R	
	D	
	V	13, 14, 37, 55, 58, 61
OL	R	
	D	57
	V	35, 45, 46, 49, 50, 51, 57
PA	R	
	D	
	V	17, 35, 43, 46, 62, 63, 65
PB	R	
	D	
	V	5, 6, 7, 10, 15, 16, 34, 49, 56, 58
PC	R	55
	D	
	V	8, 9, 39, 41, 49, 58, 61
PD	R	
	D	
	V	10, 49, 55, 56, 58, 61
PE	R	
	D	
	V	3, 14, 23, 49, 52, 58, 61, 66
PF	R	
	D	
	V	5, 6, 34, 42, 52, 55, 58, 61, 62, R15, R16
PG	R	
	D	
	V	1, 3, 36, 46, 47, 55, 58, 59

PH	R	
	D	45, 61
	V	2, 16, 40, 44, 52, 55, 57, 58, 65, 68
PI	R	
	D	57
	V	10, 18, 20, 24, 29, 30, 36, 43, 46, 55, 56, 58, 61, 66, 68
PJ	R	62
	D	38
	V	1, 12, 16, 17, 37, 40, 43, 50, 51, 58, 62
PK	R	29
	D	
	V	6, 14, 16, 17, 29, 44, 58, 61
PL	R	
	D	9
	V	2, 13, 18, 35, 37, 38, 39, 55, 58, 61, 62, 66
QA	R	56, R15
	D	
	V	1, 6, 12, 34, 39, 47, 48, 49, 52, 64, R15, R16
QB	R	
	D	3
	V	1, 2, 5, 6, 7, 8, 21, 30, 36, 46, 47, 48, 49, 52, 56, 58, 60
QC	R	
	D	
	V	8, 14, 43, 44, 45, 48, 49, 50, 51, 52, 58, 60
QD	R	
	D	
	V	6, 7, 37, 49, 52, 58, 62
QE	R	10, 13
	D	3
	V	1, 2, 3, 6, 7, 49, 52, 55, 56, 58, 65, 66, 68
QF	R	
	D	
	V	2, 47, 48, 49, 52, 58, 63, 64
QG	R	58, 59
	D	
	V	13, 14, 16, 17, 18, 40, 43, 44, 52, 55, 56, 58, 61, 68
QH	R	
	D	
	V	1, 17, 23, 39, 44, 45, 52, 55, 56
QI	R	
	D	
	V	1, 2, 7, 14, 52, 55, 58, 62
QJ	R	62
	D	
	V	1, 9, 12, 20, 41, 52, 55, 62, 63
QK	R	3, 29
	D	
	V	17, 38, 43, 48, 49, 52
QL	R	
	D	18
	V	13, 41, 42, 43, 48, 52, 56, 58, 60
RA	R	55
	D	
	V	4, 5, 7, 10, 14, 42, 49, 56, 58, 66, 67, 68
RB	R	
	D	
	V	2, 3, 4, 5, 6, 10, 22, 27, 31, 34, 49, 58
RC	R	43, 62
	D	
	V	5, 36, 39, 44, 49, 57
RD	R	55, R15
	D	
	V	1, 7, 9, 15, 16, 30, 42, 44, 46, 48, 49, 58, 59, 62. 64
RE	R	
	D	
	V	2, 4, 7, 29, 43, 45, 49, 56, 58, 60, 61
RF	R	
	D	
	V	10, 45, 49, 52, 55, 58, 59, 62, 66
RG	R	3, 58, 59
	D	5, 62
	V	1, 4, 6, 19, 47, 49, 50, 51, 52, 55, 56, 58, 64, 67
RH	R	
	D	
	V	13, 20, 27, 29, 36, 39, 44, 45, 47, 48, 52, 55, 56, 58, 60, 62, 64, 67

RI	R	R17
	D	
	V	1, 10, 20, 35, 37, 39, 49, 52, 55, 57, 58, 61
RJ	R	43, 62
	D	44
	V	15, 21, 39, 43, 56, 57, 59, 62
RK	R	4
	D	33
	V	7, 17, 19, 31, 44, 45, 47, 48, 55, 58, 59, 61, 63, 67, R15, R16
RL	R	32, 65
	D	R15
	V	13, 18, 26, 27, 30, 37, 43, 47, 50, 51, 52, 55, 56, 58, 59, 61, 65, 68, R16, R17
SA	R	
	D	
	V	5, 9, 14, 19, 34, 45, 52, 56, 61, 66, 67
SB	R	
	D	37
	V	5, 6, 7, 44, 45, 49, 52, 56, 58
SC	R	
	D	59
	V	1, 4, 8, 37, 39, 49, 56
SD	R	55
	D	62
	V	3, 5, 15, 16, 39, 41, 42, 44, 49, 56, 58, 68
SE	R	
	D	26
	V	5, 14, 29, 41, 44, 49, 50, 51, 56, 58, 66, 68
SF	R	62
	D	
	V	4, 5, 7, 41, 44, 49, 52, 55, 56, 57, 58, 59
SG	R	
	D	
	V	4, 5, 6, 7, 11, 12, 15, 16, 30, 45, 49, 50, 51, 55, 56, 60, 68
SH	R	
	D	
	V	3, 5, 16, 42, 48, 49, 55, 56, 59, R15, R16

SI	R	
	D	
	V	3, 5, 8, 17, 20, 49, 55
SJ	R	62
	D	
	V	5, 8, 19, 25, 34, 47, 55, 62
SK	R	61
	D	33, 40
	V	5, 10, 39, 49, 50, 51, 58, 59, 62, 63, R15, R16
SL	R	32, 62
	D	
	V	2, 4, 5, 14, 15, 17, 29, 33, 34, 35, 46, 49, 52, 55, 58, 59, 60, 62, 66, 67, R15, R16
TA	R	
	D	
	V	1, 6, 9, 15, 16, 33, 42, 44, 45, 46, 49, 52, 55, 56, 60, 67
TB	R	64
	D	
	V	4, 7, 16, 29, 30, 36, 38, 41, 42, 45, 46, 47, 56
TC	R	42, 64
	D	
	V	11, 12, 36, 39, 49, 56, 58, 62, R17
TD	R	5, 14, 16, 23, 25, 42, 55, 58, 64, R15
	D	
	V	11, 17, 23, 38, 41, 42, 49, 56, 57, 58
TE	R	55
	D	
	V	9, 11, 17, 18, 19, 34, 45, 49, 52, 56, 57, 58, 59, 61, 66
TF	R	59
	D	
	V	21, 42, 49, 50, 51, 52, 55, 62, 68, R17
TG	R	
	D	
	V	5, 8, 9, 10, 14, 15, 16, 29, 41, 49, 52
TH	R	
	D	R16
	V	6, 15, 19, 27, 28, 39, 40, 41, 43, 44, 46, 49, 50, 51, 56, 59, 62, 67, R15

TI *R* 58
  D R16
  V 5, 8, 10, 16, 17, 19, 20, 32,
    39, 45, 58, 59, 60, 62,
    68, R15

TJ *R* 15, 62
  D R16
  V 5, 6, 9, 13, 16, 28, 30, 31,
    41, 42, 43, 44, 50, 51, 58,
    59, 61, 62, 64, 65, R15

TK *R* 62
  D 63
  V 5, 9, 10, 17, 27, 31, 39, 43,
    49, 50, 51, 52, 58, 59,
    60

TL *R* 62, 64, 65
  D 42
  V 6, 9, 12, 16, 18, 39, 43, 48,
    55, 59, 62

Index

Addenbrooke, 10
Alphabet I, 11, 13, 14, 73
  II, 11, 13, 14, 15, 18, 28, 67, 71, 179, 184
  III, 29, 67, 68, 71, 72, 73, 75, 179, 184
  IV, 71, 172
Archer, Henry, 9, 11
  Perforation, 10, 16
  Plates handed over to, 12

Bacon, Sir E. D., 15, 102, 172, 190
Bacon, J. B., 10
Barrowman, Philips & Co., 198
Bedale, 191
Bemrose, 9
Birmingham, 14
Blueing, 28, 68, 70, 87, 172, 201, 205
Boyd, J. &. C., 195, 196
Brighton, 191
British Philatelist, 71, 195

Cameo heads, 144, 163, 167
Cancellations, duplex, 195 (see obliterations)
Cardiff Penny, 190
Cocker Bros. Ltd., 198
Constant marks, 76, 186, 190
Copestake, Moore, Crampton & Co., 195, 196
Crimea, 14

Dawbarn & Co., Wm., 198
De La Rue, 11, 205
Die I, 11, 18, 26
Die II, 18, 26, 28, 67, 72, 172, 179
Die, original, 26
Double letters, 73, 76

Eddison, Dr H. W., 5
Edinburgh, 191

217